Triangles All the Way Down

The Ubiquity of Mimesis in Life and Literature

by

Doughlas Remy

Doremiarts
MMXXI

ISBN: 9798466683738
ASIN: B09DMR9BW2

DEDICATION

To my Husband

TABLE OF CONTENTS

Chapter 5: Guilt and Innocence in Fritz Lang's Films Noirs 143

Chapter 6: Styles of Impersonation 171

Chapter 7: Pathologies 185

Triangles All the Way Down

Introduction and Acknowledgments

Mimetic theory has interested me ever since I first encountered it during my graduate studies at the University of Texas in Austin more than four decades ago. Though I had entered the program to study French and Italian, I had already realized that an understanding of languages and literatures was incomplete without knowledge of several other humanistic disciplines as well, and the scope of my interests had expanded into comparative literature, history, psychology, and anthropology. More recently, I've realized how important neuroscience and evolutionary biology were in understanding the human sciences that I started with. There was no end to it. E. O. Wilson's *Consilience: the Unity of Knowledge*, would not be published until 1998, but I could already see that everything was indeed interconnected, just as the sages have always told us.

The synergy of these accumulated interests only increased my desire for the goods that they offered. Those goods, which came in the form of memories, insights, and intuitions, were like the pieces of a jigsaw puzzle that I was trying to assemble.

Any search for knowledge is an effort of sorting, *assemblage*, categorization, ranking, and reduction. We want to know *how* seemingly unrelated phenomena are connected, to find the unity in their multiplicity and make reliable inferences from the patterns that they exhibit. Our innate capacities for searching are greatly enhanced by a secular education and the cognitive skills that it fosters.

So, in 1978, a French-American professor named René Girard visited my department as a guest lecturer from Stanford. He introduced a theory to which he himself had made groundbreaking contributions in his examinations of major literary works by Cervantes, Shakespeare, Stendhal, Flaubert, Dostoevsky, Proust, and others. The concept of mimesis already had a long history in Europe before the early modern era, when the first of these writers, Cervantes, wrote *Don Quixote*. In Classical Greece, Plato and Aristotle had recognized the role of mimesis in education and the arts, while in the Christian era, the closely-related concepts of *imago Dei* and *imitatio Dei*—both derived from Judaism, were inscribed in the teachings of Jesus and Paul the Apostle. "Be imitators of God," was Paul's exhortation to the Ephesian Christians. In the modern era, Girard's precursors include Baruch Spinoza, Anton Mesmer, Sigmund Freud, and Carl Gustav Jung.

Mimetic theory is now principally associated with Girard's name, though the list of subsequent contributors has grown very long. His earliest works—e. g., *Deceit, Desire, and the Novel* (1965) and *Violence and the Sacred* (1977), created a surge of interest in academic and intellectual circles throughout Europe and America. In 1978, he was interviewed about his theory by two French psychiatrists—Jean-Michel Oughourlian and Guy Lefort. The fruit of their collaboration was *Des choses cachées depuis la fondation du monde* (Grasset 1978). Nine years later, the English version appeared under the title, *Things Hidden Since the Foundation of the World* (Stanford, 1987). Oughourlian's contribution to this effort inspired me to delve deeper into his thinking about the psychological mechanisms of desire. Four years after his interview with René Girard, Oughourlian published *Un mime nommé désir* (1982), which appeared in English in 1991 as *The Puppet of Desire*. Two further works appeared (in French) in 2007 and 2010. The titles of their English translations are *The Genesis of Desire* and *Psychopolitics*, both published by Michigan State University Press in 2010 and 2012, respectively.

Oughourlian's work has been of particular value to me in the current phase of my research into mimetic theory and the writing of this book. His concept of interdividual psychology is grounded in neurological research around the discovery of mirror neurons in the mid-nineties, as well as more recent studies of imitation in infants. He has proposed a new psychology that takes into account the existence of a "third brain"—a mimetic brain constituted by the activity of mirror neurons. This brain's interactions with the cognitive and limbic brains are key to understanding human behavior, as I hope to show in the pages that follow.

The vast explanatory power of mimetic theory has had important implications for all the human sciences. Girard believed mimesis (imitation) to be not just integral but foundational to every aspect of human culture, from education to religion to war, and from the genesis of our species to modern times. Some scholars have characterized it a unified field theory of the human sciences—the dream of Enlightenment philosophers like Diderot and d'Alembert, whose *Encyclopédie* promised a systematic analysis of the "order and interrelations of human knowledge."

Girard's eschatology—especially his belief in the inevitability of apocalyptic violence—is a product of his later years and has so far not convinced me. Nevertheless, I am still both impressed and inspired by his earlier work in literature, anthropology, and psychology. On the matter of apocalypse, I am, at least for the present, much more in tune with "conditional optimists" like Stephen Pinker.

Early in 2021, I wrote an autobiography, *Gay Revelations*, in which I repeatedly mentioned mimetic theory in connection with my own life story. Later, a reader suggested (only half facetiously) that I author a second book to explain the first one. I decided this could be a worthwhile endeavor insofar as it would deepen my understanding of the theory and better equip me to explain it to others. I have always found writing to be a highly effective thinking process.

Despite advances in the neuroscientific understanding of mirror neurons, mimetic theory is still speculative in many areas and invites critical appraisal. At the same time, it challenges all the human sciences to rethink assumptions they may have made about the origins and mechanisms of all human culture.

Chapter Thumbnails

Chapter 1 ("The Third Brain") connects the discovery of mirror neurons to the theory that predicted it decades earlier in Girard's literary criticism. In so doing, it establishes an empirical foundation for all the later chapters.

Chapter 2 ("Mimesis") attempts to explain the core concept of mediated desire and draws examples mostly from film literature, especially, classic Hollywood and international films like *All About Eve* (1951), *Of Human Bondage* (1934), *The Talented Mr. Ripley (1999),* and *The Duellists (1977).*

Chapter 3 ("Scapegoating") explains the role of mimesis in generating and managing social tensions through ritual sacrifice, prohibitions, and myth—a triad that constitutes the Sacred.

Chapter 4 ("Representations") examines the ways in which dramatic narrative has used representation both to extend the reach of sacrificial ritual and to reveal its mechanisms.

Chapter 5 ("Guilt and Innocence in Fritz Lang's *Films Noirs*") discovers lucid depictions of sacrificial violence and the power of guilt in eight *films noirs* that were directed, scripted, or produced by Fritz Lang between 1931 and 1954, first in Germany, then in Hollywood.

Chapter 6 ("Styles of Impersonation") explores ways in which individuals, as "subjects" in the mimetic triangle, may consciously represent their models and rivals through mostly performative impersonations that include drag and satire as well as the role-playing of mainstream actors.

Chapter 7 (Pathologies) is about representations of the Other (the rival-obstacle) in various forms of neurosis and psychosis where doubling, or splitting, has occurred in the self of the subject. The chapter ends with a mimetic reading of Jules Dassin's film *Phaedra* (1962).

Film Classics Revisited

Two of Lang's earliest films, *M* and *Fury*, struck me as containing pristine examples of the kind of frenzied crowd behavior that Girard has elucidated so well throughout his work. Looking further, I found that all of Lang's films expressed certain intuitions about the mimetic linkages between desire and violence—intuitions that partly accounted for his decision to emigrate from Germany to the US in 1933 when the Nazis came to power.

Stories of human desire and conflict are over-abundant in the narrative literature of print and films. In this book, I have focused mainly on film, including the screen versions of novels. Though I recognize the risk of ignoring their authors' intentions, I wanted my applications of mimetic theory to be accessible to readers who may know these stories only as movies.

As I hope to show, all of these are about entanglements of triangular, mimetic desire. There are also references throughout this work to public figures (e.g., Donald Trump) and historical events such as the storming of the US Capitol Building on January 6, 2021. For anyone interested in the broad social and political effects of mimesis, Trump's entire presidency was a gold mine of information.

A Note on Pronouns

As an English teacher and linguist, have always struggled with the gender pronoun pairs "he or she," "him or her," and "his or her," which I find clumsy and distracting in both speech and writing.

Additionally, I find the use of "their" confusing when it replaces the more precise "his or her" or is used to indicate non-binary gender, as in these two examples:

*Although the sufferer's image may be seen by others, **they** claim not to see it.* (Who claims not to see it, the sufferer or the others?)

*"The doctor is not in **their** office. **They**'ve gone out for lunch"* (Do "their" and "they" refer to a single person or several?)

To avoid needless ambiguity, I will replace the gender pronoun pairs with "s/he" (which may be elongated in speech or pronounced *sh-he*), "himr," and "hisr." All three are intuitive, efficient, and compact, and I trust they will not be as distracting as their customary alternatives.

I will also use my collapsed gender pronoun pairs instead of the non-gendered "their" (referring to a single person). I hope these innovations will not offend other LGBTQ+ persons.

Chapter 1: The Third Brain

Mirror Neurons

In the early 1990s, a team of researchers at the University of Parma discovered what they were to call "mirror neurons" in the brains of macaque monkeys. These neurons fire roughly 300 milliseconds before the resulting motor activity is observed in the individual and are activated by the sight of another individual performing the same action. Thus, when Sue Monkey sees Joe Monkey reach for a banana—even when it is among several others within her reach—she almost simultaneously feels an impulse to reach for it as well. That autonomic impulse, originating in her mirror neurons, may translate into motor activity, or it may be blocked, delayed, or shaped by competing impulses, none of which originates in her conscious mind. If she grabs the banana, it will not be because she has consciously decided to do so.

Sue's impulse to appropriate the banana follows so closely on the heels of Joe's gesture of appropriation that neither of them can possibly know which came first. That in itself may pose no problem for them, but the very fact of their ignorance about this has become hugely significant *to us* since the discovery that much of *our* social behavior, too, is governed by mirror neurons. Studies of the behavioral implications of these neurons in our species have raised a host of questions about consciousness, responsibility, and the nature of desire. We now know that humans imitate not just others' actions but also their desires, emotions, and even their intentions, where those intentions can be inferred.

The imitation of another person's team spirit may inspire and promote cooperation, while the imitation of another's gesture of appropriation may lead to conflict. In both cases, a feedback effect may occur, whether between two mirrored individuals or throughout an entire network of them. Desires and emotions can spread virally due to the ubiquity and strength of mimesis. Cooperation generates enthusiasm, which generates even more cooperation, and conflict tends to escalate if left unchecked by compromise, concession, or intervention. But, whereas runaway cooperation is rarely a problem, runaway violence can destroy an entire community.

In human communities, runaway violence can end tragically in the death or expulsion of one or both adversaries and provoke reprisals by their allies, creating further cycles of violence that draw in everyone and threaten social order. Our species has the unique ability to annihilate ourselves under the principle of mutually assured destruction, destroying our entire ecosystem in the process. Fortunately, macaques are not highly-enough "evolved" to do such a thing. But, despite our vaunted evolutionary superiority, we are a grave danger to ourselves and our planet.

Human societies have never succeeded in eliminating violence, only in expelling it through further violence—a second, sovereign violence that is meticulously contained and ritualized so that it does not spread. In the modern world, this is the implied or actual violence meted out by sovereign states as punishment for violent crimes or as retaliation for attacks on its territory. In archaic societies around the world, domestic violence was usually managed by means of sacrifice, the violent expulsion of violence, as we shall see in the ensuing chapters.

The moment at which our primate ancestors reflexively discovered such methods of violence *management* was the moment that we became *homo sapiens*, for it signaled the birth of culture, which is definitionally concerned with the maintenance of social order through prohibitions, obligations, rituals, and the establishment of hierarchies. These developments could not have occurred without highly-evolved networks of mirror neurons working together with a highly-developed forebrain (the rational, cortical brain) and the limbic (emotive) brain.

These neurons are scattered throughout the cortical and limbic areas of human brains. They are responsible for language acquisition and cultural transmission as well as our human capacity for empathy. The malfunctioning of these neurons has been associated with autism, an inability to spontaneously and reflexively imitate others' behaviors and emotions.

Mimesis (imitation, mirroring) suffuses and encompasses every aspect of our human experience. By allowing us to "read" and interpret the complex behaviors and intentions of others, it makes flexible socialization possible to an extent that no other species can equal. It accounts for our ability to learn from others and teach them in turn. Without it, there would be no language, nor any social organization as we know it.

I have found Girard's use of a "triangular" model of desire useful in schematizing many of these concepts, and I will resort to it again and again in the pages that follow.

In Figure 1 (below), the person who is imitated (e.g., the teacher) is the "model" for the imitating "subject" (the learner). What is modeled for the subject may be a body of knowledge, a sequence of sounds or gestures, an intention, a goal, an attitude, a technique, a worldview—in short, virtually anything that can be imitated and learned. This is how knowledge spreads. And it is also how misinformation and emotions spread, for they, too, may become viral.

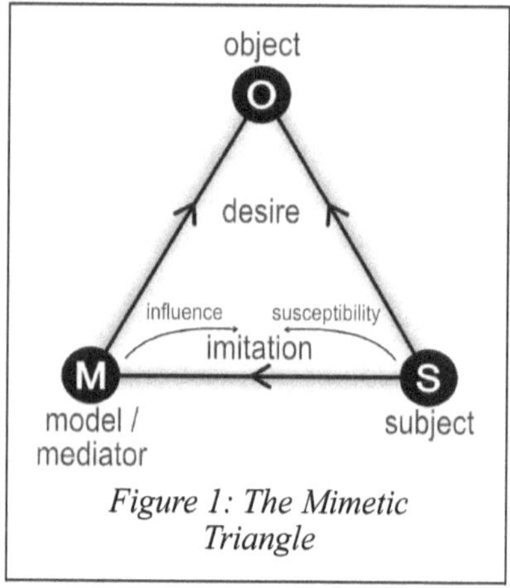

Figure 1: The Mimetic Triangle

Consider fear. Rightly or wrongly, intentionally or not, we model our fears when we share them with others, who may then either dismiss them or model them for an even wider circle of others. Contagions of fear are a value-neutral, evolutionary adaptation that allows us to coordinate our instinctual fight-or-flight responses to perceived threats. The challenge for our species has always been to distinguish between real threats and imagined ones, because contagious fear reactions—if based on misinformation or delusion—are wasteful of energy and resources—and sometimes catastrophically so, as historians of war and revolution can attest.

Multitudes of Selves

The discovery of mirror neurons was momentous in the history of neuroscience, not least because it validated the theory that René Girard had articulated in 1961 with the publication of *Mensonge romantique and vérité romanesque* (translated as *Deceit, Desire and the Novel: Self and Other in Literary Structure*). Mimetic theory had little or no basis in neuroscientific research until mirror neurons were discovered.

Prior to that discovery, neuroscience had never accounted for imitation or recognized its scope in humans. The truth is that, at any given moment and in virtually all cases, we are far, far more imitative of others than we would like to admit. If we dig deep down under the concept of vanity, we'll find delusions of autonomy, which appear necessary to hold each of us together as a "self." For philosophers, psychologists, and others, the research into mirror neurons has provided empirical support for an understanding of the "self" as a multitude of other "selves"—a kind of memory bank containing untold thousands of copies, or *re-presentations*, of the subject's impressions of hisr models over time. These models have all, without exception, *presented* themselves to himr through relationships and the media. Some are close and others are far away. Some are troublesome and others are helpful. To the extent that the subject is even aware of these influences, s/he may imagine that s/he controls them. But in fact s/he does not, because s/he is constituted *by* them. "S/he"—the self—is an illusion from the start. It exists only as a jostling multitude of others—friends, rivals, lovers, movie stars, sports heroes, fashion models, fictional characters, mentors, parents—the whole crowd of influencers past and present.

Most imitation appears to be non-conscious, making it a difficult object of study. Mimes and actors may have exquisite control over their collections of selves, but most people mistakenly—and perhaps more pragmatically—consider themselves autonomous agents interacting with other autonomous agents. Given the fact that humans are highly social animals, this illusion has probably also been adaptive, like imitation itself. The apportionment of responsibility, deterrence, punishment, and reward would be impossible without it. These are essential functions of any society, no matter how humanely punishment and deterrence are applied.

Despite the difficulty in bringing these mimetic forces into consciousness, philosophers and poets since Plato have attempted to do so. Practitioners of conscious and controlled imitation in the arts may have been the first to intuit its central role in all human social behavior. Judaism had already reckoned with it for countless generations even before Christianity carried that reckoning further. Oughourlian has made the case that the creation story in the first chapters of Genesis is about little other than mimesis. All spiritual and philosophical traditions have recognized the problematic nature of mimesis: that it accounts for both our glories and our tragedies as humans.

The Three Brains

The Venn diagram in Figure 2 (below)—an enhancement of one provided by Oughourlian in *The Mimetic Brain*—represents the brains of two individuals. In each, there are three main overlapping functions ranked in the order of their historical appearance as objects of scientific inquiry—the rational, the emotive, and the mimetic functions. In evolutionary time, however, the emotive brain preceded the other two—the rational and the mimetic—which have flowered spectacularly in our species, at least if success can be measured by capacity or potential.

Perhaps the most intriguing part of the diagram is the symbiosis at the intersection of the two mimetic brains. This is the locus of what makes us social animals—our ability to empathize, to share and enter "into" another's joys or sorrows. Empathy comes from the emotive part of the brain as a response to another's emotion—a response elicited by mirror neurons. These neurons are activated *prior to* activation of the emotive brain, which is followed by activation of the rational brain.

It's important to recognize that the rational brain does not always produce rational output. It more often supplies justifications and rationalizations for the mimetic and emotive brains. Even when particular mimetic effects are consciously identified and orchestrated, they are rarely understood. A deeper understanding of these effects may be achieved through

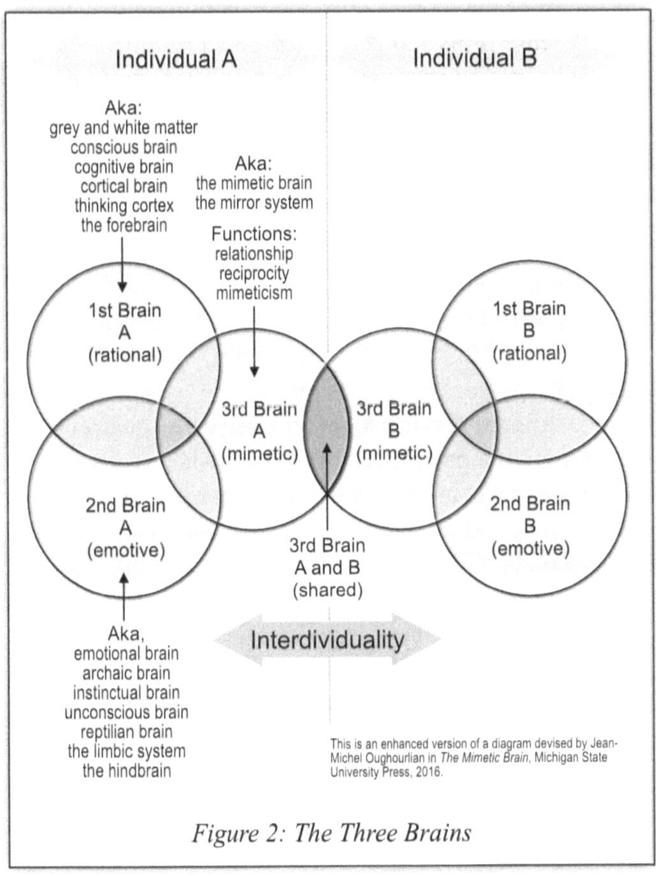

Figure 2: The Three Brains

various disciplines such as performance art, psychotherapy, and meditation.

We are born without any innate understanding of the innate workings of our brains. How could it be otherwise? The developing fetus cannot be burdened with so much cognition, and there is as yet no "self" to become its object. The "self" is formed gradually through unconscious imitation of another's desires, intentions, and goals—especially those of the mother or nurse during the earliest stages of a child's development. The infant follows the mother's gaze to find its object, then mimics the mother's emotions in finding it. The child's sense of its *self* is thus a product of mirroring and cannot be said to exist independently. There is no autonomous self, only the illusion of one, because we do not "own" our desires as we think we do, and they are not antecedent to the other's desires. The illusion of priority often leads to conflict when two or more desires converge on the same unsharable object.

In everyday life, the same mirror neurons that trigger positive emotive responses also trigger negative ones, and the "first brain"—the rational brain—doesn't always know how to head them off.

Children playing together sometimes quarrel over possession of a particular object even when replicas of that same object are freely available in the play space. One of the children picks up the object and is observed by a second child who immediately wants it more than anything in the world and claims it for himrself. "I saw it first!", each one of them cries, and their still-developing rational brains cannot listen to reason. They are not placated when a parent or teacher points out that there are enough of these objects for both of them.

The first child may have picked up the object out of curiosity or a need for physical or mental stimulation, but desire only arises in the presence of an other's desire or perceived desire—perhaps that of the teacher who has said "Oh, look! What a great toy!" or that of a third child who has reached for it. Advertising also finds fertile soil in a child's developing mind and has proven its ability to mediate the child's desires.

The webs of desire can be very hard to trace and become more and more imbricated as the child grows older. Certain models will have greater power than others to influence the child, and desires themselves can entail both attraction and avoidance. What matters for our immediate purposes is that (1) a multiplicity of models can influence a single subject, (2) a single model can influence a multiplicity of subjects, (3) no desire is autonomous, and (4) the mechanisms of desire are almost universally misrecognized.

Mimetic theory advances a narrow definition of desire, distinguishing it from needs and appetites. A hungry child will have an purely physiological appetite (and perhaps a need) for a chocolate cookie, but no desire attaches to that cookie unless it is either withheld or appropriated by another. It is then that the emotive brain becomes activated to respond with tears, supplications, and perhaps even destructive rage. In extreme cases, the subject may even destroy the object so that the rival cannot possess it. Sadly, many adults also manifest such behaviors, as we'll see in several of the films I've chosen to review.

Escalations

What to do? Escalating rivalry can lead to violence as each desire intensifies in response to the other's intensifying desire. From the playground to geopolitics, such feedback loops are threats to species survival, and both the conscious and the non-conscious brains "understand" this at a species level. The cooperation between them has been adaptive since it began, but there is still far to go. The dangers inherent in runaway violence may overtake the glacially slow evolutionary processes that curb it.

Historically, the conscious brain has been largely impotent in the face of these escalations, but the mimetic and emotive brains have devised ways of channeling the unruly passions that drive them. These remedies have used violence to contain violence. Under Sharia law, for example, adulteresses are to be publicly stoned. Jasmina Khadra's 2005 novel, *The Swallows of Kabul*, describes such a stoning that occurred when the Taliban first held power in Afghanistan. The event was held in a stadium, and the audience was encouraged to participate. As we will see in Chapter 3 ("Scapegoating"), what Khadra described was human sacrifice in the most archaic sense of the term.

The public nature of that event and the public's participation in it focus the entire population's attention on the consequences (for women) of adultery. So why is adultery prohibited? Why not just let it "play out," as we enlightened moderns do? The answer is that modern societies are much more fragmented than archaic ones, and we are largely indifferent to the domestic dramas unfolding in other families. Our indifference results from the gradual loosening of bonds of solidarity that typically held archaic societies together. As Paul Dumouchel writes in *The Ambivalence of Scarcity*, "The abandoning of obligations of solidarity makes us indifferent to conflicts and violence that do not concern us directly." Formerly (and still, in most traditional societies), when there was a conflict of any kind— especially one involving proscribed sexual relationships—everybody knew about it and everybody got involved and took sides. What began as a spark could quickly become a conflagration.

The ages-old prohibition against adultery is designed to prevent rivalrous and violent conflict between men. A married or betrothed woman is a possession that cannot be shared—and not just any possession, but one that generates value through domestic labor, the production of children, and the formation of alliances. Under Taliban rule as described in Khadra's story, the severity of the punishment for adultery is a warning to all women and girls that violations of a husband's rights to their bodies will not be tolerated and that they alone are responsible for upholding the prohibition. Modern Afghanistan is not nearly as "archaic" as the Taliban would like it to be, and the realities of the modern world may eventually prevail.

The scale of this problem has always been monumental. Early hominids might well have self-destructed without evolutionary adaptations that gave our species the means of managing, if certainly not eliminating, its violence. These adaptations are collectively known as culture—the social structurings that, paradoxically, use violence to keep violence at bay—much like a poison that is also used as a cure. These structurings are common to every society and rely on the efficacy of various forms of sacrifice with their attendant rituals, myths, and prohibitions. The repository of these forces is the Sacred, symbolized not only by the Ark of the Covenant, the Kaaba, the Bible, and the Koran—but also by the ostensibly "secular" structurings and symbologies of sovereign states as established in their constitutions, their hallowed spaces, their protocols, and their traditions.

The linkage of children's playground quarrels with fundamental human institutions such as religion may seem improbable, but the human sciences—particularly philosophy, literary studies, anthropology, evolutionary biology, and neuropsychology—have long acknowledged their connection.

Emotions, Moods, and Feelings

In humans, the second brain (the limbic system governing emotions, feelings, and moods) is not the prime mover as it is in cats and lizards. When sensory input from another individual is incoming, our third (mimetic) brain gets there first, our second (emotive) brain arrives second, and our first (rational) brain comes in last. Typically, as in the case of cognitive biases, the first brain does nothing more than rationalize and justify what the other two brains have already decided. As one's sense of self is fashioned out of perceived differences between oneself and others, the first brain functions to misrecognize the interdividual relation for what it is—a zone of contested identity where ownership and priority—if not clearly established from the outset—are sorted out through negotiation or violence. Sometimes the negotiating process unfolds over years and is so subtle as to be unnoticed, and, in other cases, it is immediate and noisy. It can be either productive or destabilizing. The key to its success is the avoidance of runaway violence that affects everyone.

Like human brains, the brains of cats and lizards also prioritize identification over emotions. Hormones like adrenalin and oxytocin are not released into the blood stream until the "other" (creature) has been identified and ranked as prey, predator, or neither. These biochemical responses are driven primarily by instinct, not mediated by the interdividual rapports of any third brain or the rationalizations provided by a first brain.

EMOTIONS

Emotions like fear and rage are primal, but at the human level, they may also be aroused mimetically. Political and religious demagogues are notoriously adept at modeling paranoia and outrage for the masses, whose susceptibility can only be understood as a function of the mimetic rapports among everyone involved, paired with their first brains' failures to recognize those rapports.

The strength of these rapports is entirely dependent on their misrecognition by the conscious mind. Except in theatre, one cannot simply mimic an irrational fear while recognizing its true source. To do so would be tantamount to admitting that one's fear has been enlisted, co-opted, and shaped not by one's "own" self but by a controlling and manipulative Other. Without an accompanying recognition of the true origin of that fear, the subject's sense of self cannot hold, for it is based on the presumption of autonomy and difference. Knowledge of the reality that one's desires and thus one's self are not truly one's own directs the subject down one of three paths. The first leads to wisdom and requires a tempering of the mimetic and emotional brains by the rational brain. The second leads to neurosis, the deployment of defense mechanisms (e.g., phobias) and hysteria to reclaim ownership of one's desires. The third leads to psychosis, which claims the antecedence and priority of one's desires over the Other's, resulting in all manner of delusions about that rapport.

The more positive emotions like joy and happiness operate in much the same way as fear and anger. They are rooted in our DNA but may be both shaped and triggered by mimesis.

MOODS

Moods are governed by genetically-programmed neurotransmitters (dopamine, noradrenaline, and serotonin) and cover the gamut from manias and euphoria to depression and lethargy. Endogenous mood patterns, including disorders, are usually hereditary and issue from the second, emotive brain. However, they attach themselves to the interdividual rapports mapped out in the third (mimetic) brain and then look to the first (cognitive) brain for religious, ethical, economic, and political justifications. The exogenous moods include those produced by trauma or exogenous chemical substances such as anti-depressants and cocaine. Whatever their causes, reactive depressions and manias manifest in the subject as troubled relationships beset by abnormally low or high affect or by alternations between the lows and the highs.

FEELINGS

Feelings like love and tenderness, hatred, envy jealousy, and resentment may be adumbrated, or foreshadowed, in certain mammals, but they come into their full glory in humans. Every one of those feelings implies the presence of another individual, and in the last four, that individual is a rival. Once again, rivalry may exist between single individuals, individuals and groups, or groups and other groups. The term "rival" simply refers to a position in the mimetic triangle of subject, model-then-rival, and object. As we shall see in the following chapters, these three positions are dynamic and dialectical: the polarity of subject and model may be relatively stable and productive, as we find in tutorial and mentoring relationships; it may deteriorate into a relation of reciprocal or non-reciprocal rivalry like that between Margo and Eve in the 1950 movie *All About*

Eve (see Chapter 2); or it may collapse into a pathological merging of subject and model/rival in which the former experiences (but cannot acknowledge) the latter as an intractable obstacle. In some cases, the Other's being is what the subject desires, but the Other will not relinquish it, so the subject desires it even more—a cycle that can only produce resentment and malice in the desiring subject. In other cases, the Other attempts to drive out the subject's desire and replace it with hisr own through a pattern of psychological or physical abuse. The subject may react by splitting into two selves—one of which s/he has relinquished to the rival-obstacle-tormenter and can no longer feel.

Relational Psychoanalysis

I noted earlier that Girard's contribution to mimetic theory predated the discovery of mirror neurons by three decades. It also predated the appearance of relational psychoanalysis. In 1983, Jay Greenberg and Stephen A. Mitchell published *Object Relations in Psychoanalytic Theory* (Harvard University Press), which elevated the importance of relationships over what Freud had identified as "drives." However, their theory carried forward from Freudian psychoanalysis two important but flawed assumptions. The first was that the analysand's current mental disorders are reenactments of relational conflicts experienced in early childhood. The second was that the two (or more) subjects (or "selves") in that earlier relationship were always distinct.

Mimetic theory rejects those two assumptions and proposes that (1) the analysand's current disorders are not reenactments of earlier events but instead manifestations of current relational conflicts involving rivalry between the resident selves, even those that are modeled on adversaries long since departed; and that (2) the "self" does not come into being until it is in relation with another self. The noun "subject," in the sense that we are using it, implies an asymmetrical relationship of dependency, tutelage, and bonding through imitation of a model. The subject (e.g., a student) is bound to the model (e.g., a professor) by their joint commitment to fulfilling their roles.

There cannot be a subject without a model, or vice versa, just as there cannot be an up without a down or an inside without an outside. The two positions are complementary and interdependent as long as the model does not also become a rival and an obstacle. When that happens, they are undifferentiated and may attempt to restore their difference (their hierarchy) through a variety of means ranging from ritualized contest (e.g., games) to verbal and physical violence.

Desire Fails Where It Succeeds

When the desiring subject succeeds in claiming the object designated to himr by the rival, disappointment often follows. This happens for a couple of reasons.

First, the perceived value of the object has been inflated by the convergence of competing desires for it. Once the rival is subdued, the object's value deflates somewhat.

Second, desire is never satisfied. One can never have enough fame, prestige, or money. So desire always looks to the same rival for another object or seeks out another model-*cum*-rival-*cum*-obstacle to designate one. Why doesn't the subject choose an object of hisr own instead? Because, in reality, no object of desire can remain desirable when others do not desire it. If the object can be easily had, there is no reason to desire it. The subject's desire comes into being in response to the desire of the other, the model. There is no desire without modeling and, potentially, rivalry. Rivalry occurs when the subject mimics the desire of a model for an unsharable object and both are unwilling to forfeit it.

The Stamp of Prestige

"What the collectors are after is a stamp where the story is known, which has been in some of the most famous collections. By buying them, their name will live on for as long as people continue to collect stamps.

"When you have two real collectors and only one item, they are going to throw everything at it."

Hugh Jefferies of Stanley Gibbons.

Possibly the world's most famous and valuable stamp is the One-Cent Magenta, printed in British Guiana in 1856. In 2014, millionaire Stuart Weitzman bought it for $9.5 million. Before reselling it in 2021, Weitzman followed the usual practice of inscribing his initials on its back. They will carry his name into the future for as long as the stamp is valued.

The stamp is indeed unique, as are many neglected relics of its era, but its appearance is unexceptional and its historical significance negligible.

Of course, such purchases may be made for any number of reasons having to do with financial management—Weitzman is not just throwing money into the wind. But Weitzman is also an enthusiastic, life-long philatelist, so we can probably assume that he was thrilled to be in possession of it. We're unlikely ever to know if he experienced buyer's remorse.

Nevertheless, the intrinsic value of the One-Cent Magenta (as opposed to its monetary value) is hard to locate in any description of it. It may be famous, unique, and valuable, but it is neither beautiful nor functional and has no real story to tell. It is hard to imagine that the pleasure of owning it is worth $9.5 million.

It's famous, yes, because every philatelist and dealer knows about it.

It's unique, yes, but so is every human being.

It's supremely valuable, yes, but only because so many philatelists want to possess it. The synergy of all those desires bids up the stamp's prestige and its monetary value, and the game is on.

It is a game for those wealthy enough to play it. Its goal is not to possess the desired object but to be *the one* who possesses it—i.e., the victor—and the prize for victory is not the trophy but the prestige that it confers on its winner.

Chapter 2: Mimesis

Plato and Aristotle

Imitation is natural to man from childhood, one of his advantages over the lower animals being this, that he is the most imitative creature in the world, and learns at first by imitation. (Aristotle)

Our human capacity for imitation, or mimesis, has been a subject of interest to philosophers and literary theorists since Plato, who believed that "ideas," or "forms," were the ultimate reality, and the material world could only offer copies, or imitations, of them. He considered art as *only* an imitation of the material world—not of the world of ideas or forms directly. Accordingly, he declared mimesis to be "the mother of all lies" and banished it from his ideal Republic.

His pupil Aristotle had a much more positive view of mimesis, regarding it as a human instinct that enables language acquisition and cultural transmission. His conception of mimesis was therefore very close to our own, which has been nurtured by the sciences. He agreed with Plato that art was a form of imitation, but whereas Plato stressed the "copying" aspect of mimesis in art, Aristotle recognized mimesis as a symbolic "re-presentation" of the world as it is, as it is believed to be, or as it ought to be. People enjoy narrative poetry, he said, because they identify with the characters and situations that it represents. This mimetic response to the re-presentation explains why narrative poetry is capable of evoking feelings of sympathy, anger, or joy in audiences. For Aristotle, this was its strength, for he regarded catharsis as ennobling rather than dangerous.

The Mimetic Triangle

Schematically, every act of modeling, whether conscious or not, involves a mimetic relation between a subject and a model with respect to an object. That object, or goal, may be mastery of a skill, a technique, or a subject matter—or it may be something more abstract, like status, participation, political power, states of mind (fear, joy, trust), or health. Or one may want to possess something of a material nature—a cookie, a lover, wealth, or property. Understandably, such a variety of object types, when multiplied by the variety of ways in which human subjects and models approach them, produces complex and sometimes unruly processes of social ordering.

Non-Reciprocal (Asymmetrical) Modeling

MICHAEL JORDAN AND THE NIKE SHOE

Every action we undertake is guided by a particular configuration of goals that may vary from moment to moment, depending on our assessment of available models and the goals they propose to us. When Michael Jordan holds out a Nike shoe to us and says simply, "Be like me," he is modeling his desires for us to imitate *non-conflictually*, as Nike shoes are mass-

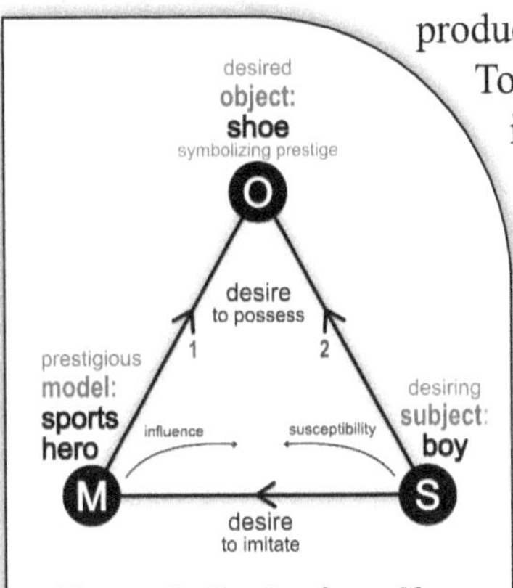

Figure 3: Desire for a Shoe

produced and mass marketed. To be "like" Michael Jordan is to desire what he desires. As a celebrated athlete, he is already a powerful role model for many boys, and in such ads he leverages this power by showing them how, by simply buying a pair of shoes, they can partake in his prestige (aka, mana or aura). Whether or not they take the bait will depend on their hierarchy of goals and/or their awareness of the manipulations in progress.

Jordan's prestige derives from his superior performance as a basketball player, but prestige may be based on any number of superior attributes or accomplishments, such as wealth, power, talent, age, expertise, and fame.

NON~RECIPROCAL MODELING FOR MULTIPLE SUBJECTS

Expanding the scope of the triangle from Figure 3, Figure 4 shows multiple triangles formed when multiple subjects imitate the desire of a single model for a single object. Figure 5 (following page) takes into account the modeling that each subject does for other

Figure 4: Multiple Subjects, One Model, and One Shoe

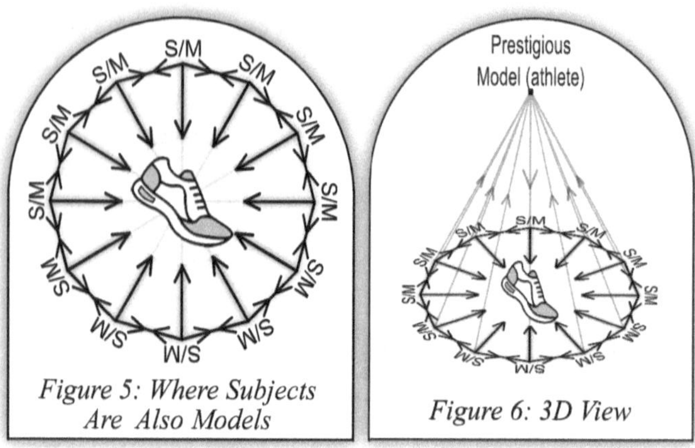

*Figure 5: Where Subjects
Are Also Models*

Figure 6: 3D View

subjects, making each of them both a model and a
subject.

Both these scenarios reflect the way in which the
Nike ad works in real life, because the multiple subjects
in Figure 3 are simultaneously copying each other's
desires as well as Michael Jordan's, as reflected in
Figure 4. Figure 6 may be helpful in visualizing these
two models simultaneously cranking out desire for the
shoe. Each sector of this 12-sided pyramid is a three-
sided one. This shows the persistence and
indispensability of the triangle in modeling desire. The
modeling in this diagram is both reciprocal (between the
subjects-*cum*-models) and non-reciprocal (between each
subject and the prestigious model).

MIMESIS AND COMMUNITY NORMS

A mentoring relationship can be said to be
"successful" if the subject has made the necessary
identification with the mentor and met the expected goal
of achievement and performance, regardless of the
merits of the goal.

But the goal, or objective, always has a social
valence that reflects the social benefits or liabilities that
result from achieving the goal, possessing the object, or

meeting the objective. The qualifiers "good" and "bad" are often attached to the word "mimesis" to indicate its social value.

Whether Michael Jordan's Nike ad amounts to either "good" or "bad" mimesis is a matter of opinion, but examples of starkly "bad" mimesis are abundant in our world, resulting in drug abuse, gang violence, and Ponzi schemes. This is why one's choice of both objects and models must be guided by consciousness of mimetic influences.

In Christianity and tribal cultures like the one from which it emerged, objects of desire are ranked by their compliance with tribal prohibitions and obligations as passed down through tradition and spelled out in sacred texts.

In a world shaped by science, objects of desire (called "objectives") are ranked by their compliance with rational and pragmatic criteria such as "do-able" and "desirable." What is deemed desirable also undergoes a ranking process that rests on shared values, and those values will hopefully have been shaped by careful thought rather than autonomous mimetic processes.

PRESTIGE

The power to influence young consumers, as Michael Jordan has done, depends on the model's prestige in the eyes of the desiring subject. And what is prestige but a measure of the subject's admiration for the model—an admiration that is itself mimetically induced? Although I recognize Jordan's immense fame and his accomplishments, I do not idolize him as many young men do. Since I am much older than they, decidedly less athletic, and thankfully more hardened against the allurements of advertising, Jordan's ad does not inspire me to buy a pair of Nike sports shoes. They do not even show up in my hierarchy of goals.

But virtually every one of my higher-level goals—those not related to survival alone—has been modeled for me at some point in my life. I learned to play the piano because certain pianists modeled for me their enjoyment of playing, the community modeled its admiration of accomplished pianists, and my piano teachers modeled their skill and knowledge. None of that could have occurred without mimesis. Nor could any other part of my education have done so. All learning involves such identifications.

The role of the mediator (or model, mentor) is of the greatest importance, for the subject does not know what to desire and must look to a teacher, a sports hero, a parent, an ideology, or an institution for help. Goals—the objects of both our appetites and desires—must be continually assessed, sorted, repositioned, promoted, demoted, divested, or purged—all in the interests of optimizing the use of our energies for the challenges of survival. Always in flux, they do not always balance out on their own or receive reliable input from the conscious brain.

CHARISMA AND CULTS

The relationship between a charismatic leader and hisr subject(s), or follower(s), may be based on shared delusions that are yet mimetically induced by the leader. Alternatively, the subjects' delusions may be induced by a non-delusional leader as a strategy of manipulation. The members of the People's Temple, who perfectly mimicked the delusions of their leader, Jimmy Jones, and committed mass suicide in Jonestown, Guyana in 1978, are of the first type. That tragedy and a similar one in San Diego County in 1997 became case studies in the power of charismatic modeling. So, too, has the cult of Trump, though the authenticity of his delusions are suspect considering the influence that Roy Cohn, a serial liar, exerted on him during his formative years. (See below.) However, there is no reason why the Donald couldn't be both delusional and a liar and master manipulator. This could be a symptom of the third brain's subversion of the first brain's role in processing and interpreting sensory input from the real world.

Reciprocal (Symmetrical) Modeling

In Figure 3, where we saw Michael Jordan modeling his desire for the shoe, only one arrow appears at the base of the triangle, pointing from the subject (the boy) toward the model (< only), indicating non-reciprocal modeling. In Figure 7 (showing Trump, his supporters, and power), the arrows at the base of the triangle (> <) indicate reciprocal mimetic influence.

Reciprocal modeling does not preclude non-reciprocal modeling in a multifaceted phenomenon like the Trump cult. Through mimesis, Donald Trump strategically aligned his interests with those of populist nationalists, white supremacists, and white evangelicals. He made their desires his own. And, again through mimesis (modeling by personal example and in speeches), he manipulated their behavior, promising them what they desired in return for their unwavering loyalty to him. What they desired ranged from unobstructed political influence to lynchings. He copied their desire and added one more—a desire for the narcissistic inflation

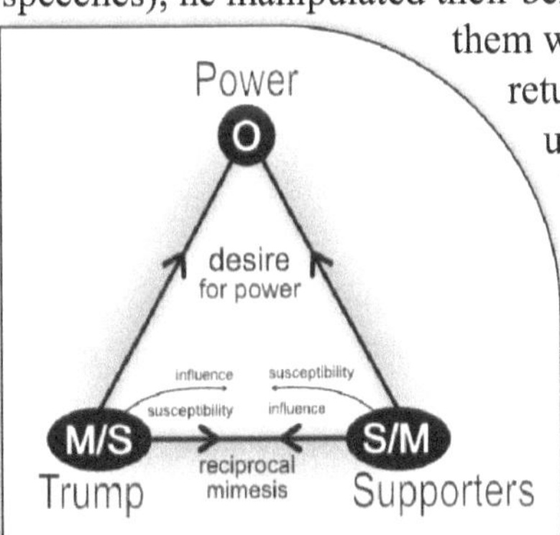

Figure 7: Reciprocal Modeling

that comes with autocratic control of a nation and its resources.

These two desires were fundamentally the same despite their differences. Instrumentally, both were directed toward untrammeled political power—power that is unconstrained by law or community norms and that may at any time declare a "state of exception" in order to to control or eliminate political enemies.

In this variation of the basic triangle, a charismatic leader and hisr supporters (the model and the subject) are jointly working toward the same goal—a goal that must be shared between them because they are mutually dependent. Neither the model nor the subject can appropriate that object without the other's help. This dynamic tilts their relationship toward complete mutual identification—the fusion of leader and followers—provided that all competing identifications are successfully backgrounded or eliminated. This is what all autocracies want but seldom achieve—especially in states with large and diverse populations.

The relationship between Trump and MAGA Nation was cult-like in its strong and *exclusive* mutual identifications, its insularity, and its disregard for community norms. When untrammeled political power is one's supreme objective, those norms are always at risk.

Acquisitive Mimesis and Mass Marketing

Mass marketing works by showing us—directly or through proxies—what we can or "should" desire in the domains of services (e.g., travel destinations, restaurants) and manufactured goods such as clothing, cars, and beverages. The advertiser mediates between us and the object of desire, and s/he does not stand in our way if we reach out to acquire that object. This is the triangle of Michael Jordan, the boy, and the shoe.

Acquisitive mimesis becomes conflictual when the object is one-of-a-kind, like *objets d'art*, or scarce, like water, or even symbolic, like soccer balls (Figures 8 and 11). Sports competitions that involve two teams pursuing a ball or disk of some kind are evidence that the desired object functions only as a symbol of prestige. It is not kept in a vault after each game.

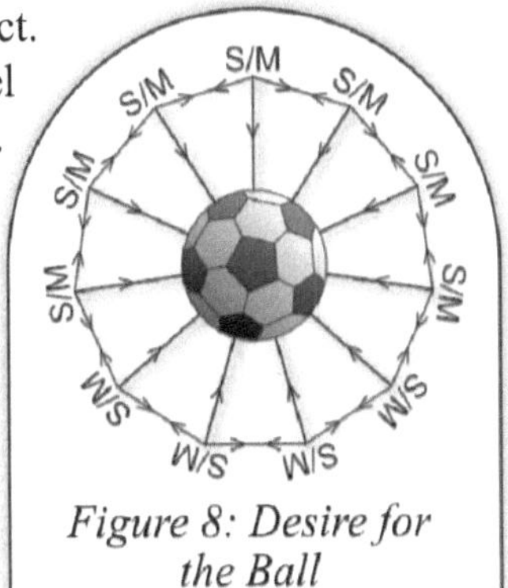

Figure 8: Desire for the Ball

The engine that drives mass marketing is mimesis. I will perhaps purchase a particular bottle of wine because my desire for it has been modeled for me directly through advertising, or indirectly through the influence of a proxy— someone whose judgment I trust—and my appreciation of it may even be influenced by hisr own. Mimetic desire can lead to sound decisions, like purchasing fair-trade chocolates, or harmful ones, like using hydroxychloroquine to fight COVID-19 or refusing to get vaccinated. All mass follies are propelled by these mimetic forces, and what makes them follies is not mimesis itself but rather the misrecognitions abetted by the first brain.

Our goals are no less compelling to us than are the Nike shoes to the young athlete. We pursue many of them with a fervor that can lead us both to glory and to defeat.

Renunciation

But why must the subject desire anything to begin with? Isn't it possible to renounce desire, as some monastic orders encourage their members to do?

Certain desires may be suppressed, but others will remain and fill their space. If one's goal is to rid oneself of all desires, that goal itself represents nothing more than one desire prioritized over all others. It is a meta-desire, a desire to live without desire, and it may be welcomed as a spiritual discipline.

The monk's willingness to chop wood and carry water indicates that he has both an ultimate goal (e.g., wisdom, peace, contributing to a collective effort) and a proximate one (preparing fuel for the fire). In mimetic terms, those goals are the objects of his desire(s). As humans, we are desiring beings because we are intensely *social* beings who interact mimetically through symbolic language and behavior. We imitate others' desires just as we imitate their gestures, their language, and their lifestyles. The mimetic triangle is dynamic and cannot be switched off. It is like the blood coursing through our veins. It's not something we can give up for Lent.

Dynamism

No diagram can ever map the complexity and flux of these processes. The diagrams that I have assembled are meant to show the underlying unity of the mimetic triangles that generate culture.

Desire Layered Over Appetites

Assuming that Betty Boop may select only *one* of the 12 suitors crowded around her, the scenario in Figure 9 seems ripe for rife rivalry. What's driving their interest in her is biological appetite, over-laid by mediated desire.

Appetites are not contagious, but desires are. Preferences for essential items like food, sex, and even water can be shaped by mimesis even when the need for them is not. The enhanced value of certain foodstuffs does not always reflect enhanced quality, and some products are purchased solely for the prestige they confer on the owner. This can be true of anything that can be possessed, whether it's a bottle of Champagne, a Warhol silkscreen, a company's shares, or a trophy wife.

Why is the trophy wife desirable? It is because other men desire her. Her husband needs *their* desire to sustain or supercharge his own. The more of them are attracted to her, the more prestige accrues to him as the champion in the contest for her affections. A male's status among other males is certain to affect his prospects in life.

Men who court women *solely* to use them as trophies—whether as wives or consorts—may be rare, but they are at only one point on a spectrum of ways in which men regard their wives and lovers.

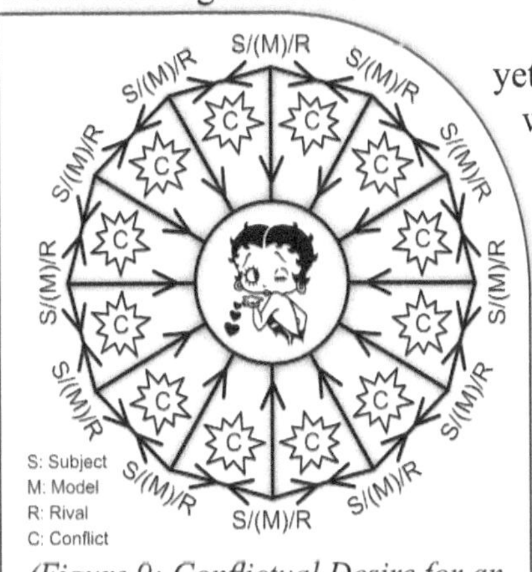

(Figure 9: Conflictual Desire for an Unsharable Object)

Betty Boop is not yet a trophy wife, but we can be sure that the successful suitor will consider her, at the very least, a trophy.

The volatility of this scenario cannot be ignored. The suitors' desires are amplified by the feedback loop inherent in symmetrical modeling even when the object is sharable. But here the object is not sharable, and these suitors are obliged to compete with each other for it. What ensues may range from a bidding war to a brawl, but it will illustrate the way in which a model becomes a rival.

Both the intensity of the rivalry and its outcome depend on a huge number of background variables that are themselves mimetic in nature. Without question, the suitors' interactions in this scenario will be conflictual as long as their desires are mediated by the other suitors. The only question is, to what extent?

Homoeroticism in the Triangle

Those familiar with Tennessee Williams' *Suddenly Last Summer* (1958) will understand how the trophy wife's *allure* sometimes functions when her husband uses her as *a lure*. (Both words are from Old French *aleurier*, to attract.)

As a subject in the mimetic triangle, Sebastian's desire for his wife Catherine is metaphysical and culturally determined, with little or no basis in appetite. He finds her desirable only in the aesthetic sense, and his aesthetic of female desirability is modeled on that of heterosexual males that he has observed. Their desire for Catherine, unlike Sebastian's, *does* have a strong basis in appetite, while *his* appetite for *her* is only thinly layered with desire.

Catherine's presence is useful to Sebastian because she attracts men's attention, which he wants for himself. His tragedy is that he cannot fuse the real object of his appetites (intimacy with another male) with its pretend-object, his trophy wife. This does not make Sebastian a villain or a pervert. He is in fact a victim of a society that cannot tolerate his proclivities. He may care

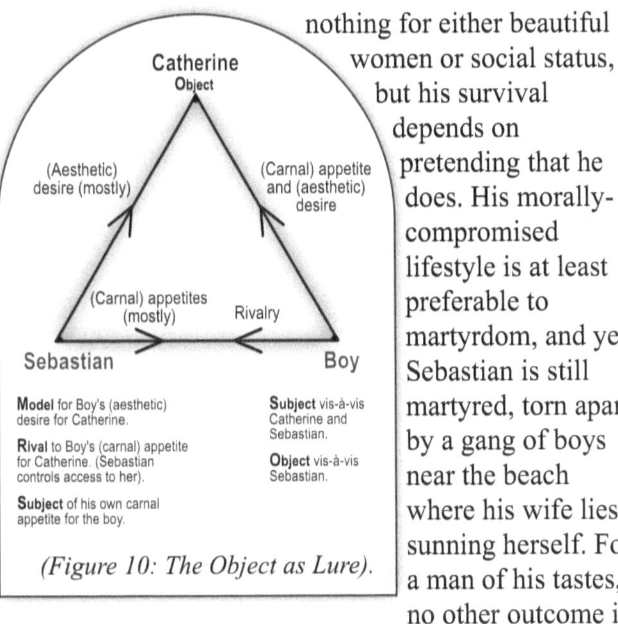

(Figure 10: The Object as Lure).

nothing for either beautiful women or social status, but his survival depends on pretending that he does. His morally-compromised lifestyle is at least preferable to martyrdom, and yet, Sebastian is still martyred, torn apart by a gang of boys near the beach where his wife lies sunning herself. For a man of his tastes, no other outcome is possible. He is the outsider, marked for sacrifice just as Hans Beckert is in Fritz Lang's *M* (see Chapter 5).

Collective Efforts to Appropriate the Object

In Figures 8 and 9, we saw conflictual desire for an unsharable object (Betty Boop and the football). In Figure 11 (below), the object is still unsharable, but here the mimetic conflict is framed, organized, and managed as a ritual event. What's new here is the collaboration within each team to appropriate the desired object for the team as a body. The conflict is only between the teams, and it is governed by rules. Each team member is both a subject and a mediator, both acting out and modeling hisr desires, which are in turn modeled for himr by the coaches and the fans. The object and its surrogates—the

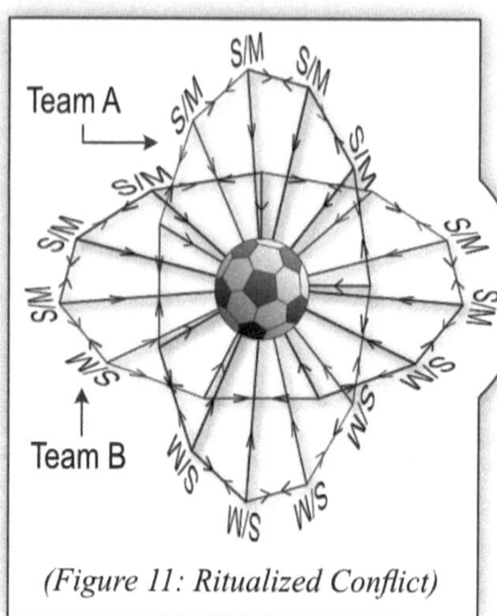

(Figure 11: Ritualized Conflict)

goal, the trophy, and the acclaim of the crowd—are purely symbolic and without any intrinsic value, and—unless the team is professional—there's no monetary reward for winning. The trophy will not be made of precious metals, the soccer ball will not become the property of either team, and the crowds may be fickle. The trophy and the ball are manufactured objects that anyone may acquire.

The thrill of the game comes from releasing aggression in a bounded, ritualized environment where it can—theoretically, at least—be managed without the risk of veering toward cruelty and disregard for life. But outside the boundaries of the game, soccer hooligans remind us what happens when aggression is *not* ritually managed.

The purpose of this particular type of ritual (also enacted in basketball, rugby, and virtually every other competitive game) is to channel aggression, both on the playing field and off. In developmental terms, the game ritual is an indispensable form of discipline, teaching self-control and respect for the rules.

A Triangle for Two

A familiar scene in period romances portrays the initial moments of a courtship in which a lady exhibits her charms to a gentleman who is obviously susceptible to them—and vice versa, for the lines from influence to susceptibility run in both directions—and there is a strong component of sexual appetite in their reciprocal desires.

So, until a rival appears, there doesn't appear to be a triangle. However,

(Figure 12: Mimetic Triangle without a Third Party)

there is a negotiation under way, for the parties in the fledgling romance inevitably have different sets of terms and objectives for the relationship. She must not yield too soon, and he must impress her to the point that she eventually does yield, but without rushing her and appearing too greedy for her love.

Both the lady and the gentleman are desiring subjects, and each is the object of the other's desire. But each must also double as a rival—blocking unwelcome moves by the other—as well as an inhibitor blocking any moves that might set him back. The inhibitor, one might say, is learned manners. He wants to possess her—mind, body and soul—but she is perhaps hesitant to cede any of those goods to him. Her desire for him is tempered by her need to preserve her honor and not appear too "easy." Each of the lovers' inhibitors acts as a rival and an obstacle, restricting access to the object. The act of love is all about greater access and the possibility of fusion. The more it is withheld, the more it is desired.

What I have described is a mimetic triangle without a third party. Each of the two lovers is simultaneously a subject, a model/rival/obstacle, and an object of desire for the other.

THE COQUETTE

Another variety of the two-party triangle involves the manipulation of one lover's desire by the other through modeling. The coquette desires herself because she has copied the desire of her lover. In so doing, she also models her desire for herself, thereby augmenting *his* desire. Knowing better than he that desire feeds on obstacles to its satisfaction, she feigns indifference, for she would have him think that she desires only herself—i.e., that she is autonomous, lacking nothing, the sole proprietor of her own

Figure 13: The Coquette

desires. Her cold indifference fascinates him and makes her seem all the more desirable—a divine essence, a goddess who possesses what he lacks and needs so badly.

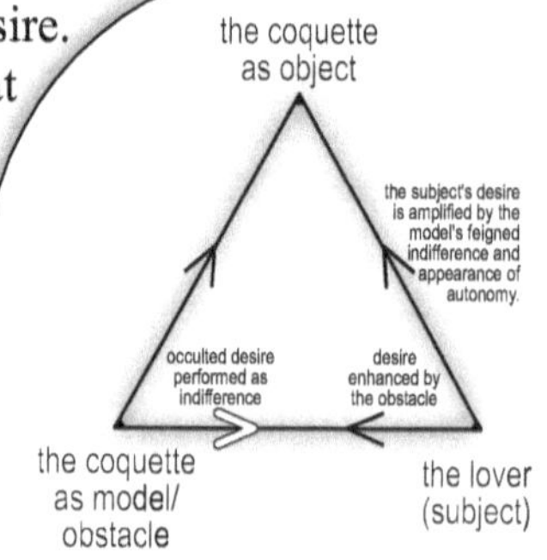

This is another instance of double mediation, one that Girard calls a "politics" of desire. It amounts to staging a desire for oneself, performing indifference, and thereby seducing the other. In Girard's words, "the secret of success, in politics as in love, is dissimulation."

For the "serial" coquette, dissimulation is a way of life, and the consequences can be tragic for everyone involved, as exemplified in Emile Zola's 1880 novel, *Nana. Of Human Bondage*, which I will review later in this chapter, also grasps these dynamics between lovers when one of them is a serial coquette.

External Mediation

René Girard refers to mimesis of the type illustrated in Figure 3 (re: Michael Jordan's Nike shoe)) as "external mediation." Though the boy is fascinated by his model, his dominant fascination is with the object that the model has designated as desirable. Because the gazes of both the model and the subject are ultimately directed *outward* toward an external object that is freely available to both, there is no rivalry, and thus no conflict.

If there were only one shoe to be had, there would still be no rivalry because of the hierarchical distance between the subject and the model, as measured by their relative prestige. The boy *cannot* be a rival to the sports hero, because the latter's aura is too powerful and the boy's susceptibility to it is too strong.

If a poor man desires possession of a Van Gogh, he is hardly in a position to bid for it. He may resent the painting's eventual owner for being wealthy enough to buy it, but unless he is irrational, the owner will not become an obstacle and then a rival to him, for he will have realized that his only obstacle is his poverty. We will shortly examine several scenarios in which the subject—not content to either renounce hisr desires or continue to stew in hisr resentments—seeks to appropriate the object despite the resistance of the model/obstacle, who, at the very least, becomes a serious rival to himr. When the subject comes to regard the object's owner as an evil enemy to be feared and destroyed, then external mediation has become internal and may result in hallucinations, a condition known as "doubling."

Internal Mediation

For Girard, external mediation is preferable to internal mediation, in which subject and model become rivals for an object that they either cannot or do not wish to share (e.g., the attentions of a mother and wife, an award, a job, a painting, a territory). Internal mediation occurs as the subject ascends closer to the model in the hierarchy of prestige and challenges hisr dominance. This may happen naturally, as when children become adults, or intentionally, as when they become experts in their fields. We may observe this pattern in every sphere of life, perhaps most conspicuously in relationships between parents and children, teachers and students, and performers and their understudies. Sometimes the model is gracious in ceding hisr place to the rival, and sometimes not, but the proximity of the two creates a potential for conflict.

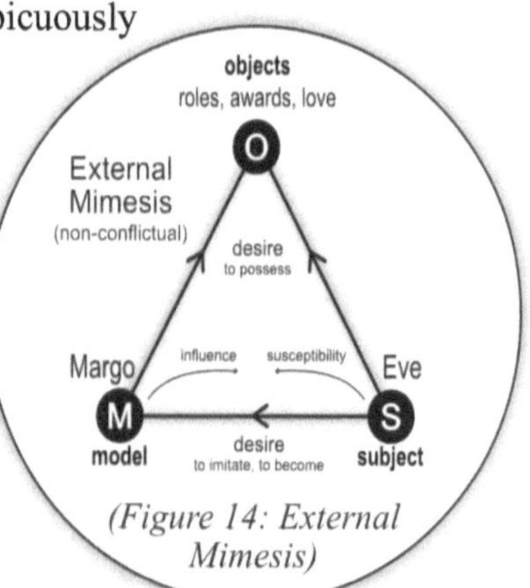

(Figure 14: External Mimesis)

DOUBLING: OBSESSIVE INTERNAL MEDIATION

When the rivals reach an impasse and neither of them will cede to the other, the intensity of their desires may provoke conflict, in which case they may quite literally characterize their adversaries as demons or animals. These characterizations are not always as metaphorical as the adversaries like to pretend. "Oh, you can't have taken me seriously!", says the challenger who has been called out for a pattern of verbal abuse that includes dehumanizing epithets like "dog," "vermin," "snake," and the like. It's clear that the abuser intends to model for hisr audience a contempt for the adversary that amounts to dehumanization.

From External to Internal Mediation

The 1953 film *All About Eve,* directed by Joseph Mankiewicz, brings these dynamics into sharp focus as few other films have done. What begins as a healthy external mediation in the relationship between a mentor and subject becomes internalized to the point that they are rivals.

(Figure 15: Internal Mimesis

Margo Channing (played by Bette Davis) is a brilliant and famous—but aging—Broadway stage actress engaged to Bill, her director (Gary Merrill). One evening, after her performance, she is approached in her dressing room by a much younger woman of humble appearance (Eve Harrington, played by Anne Baxter), who passionately professes her admiration for everything that Margo is and does. Margo, susceptible as she is to such ardent displays of adoration, takes an interest in Eve and hires her as a personal assistant, never imagining that she might soon become a rival. Eve's fascination with Margo is the kind of strong identification that occurs naturally in mentoring relationships, where the subject learns by imitating the model, then catches up with or surpasses the model, and then becomes a model himrself. This is what Eve intends, and she is a very quick study.

Because Eve is copying Margo's desires, she seems intent on acquiring for herself the two unsharable objects that Margo desires the most—her preeminence (as measured by roles, awards and public adulations) and her fiancé, Bill. Eve relies on her youth, her beauty, and her moral flexibility to ensure those two outcomes. This is the stage at which Margo becomes an *obstacle* to Eve.

Eve's intentions become increasingly transparent to Margo when Bill appoints Eve to be her understudy. The two actresses are now rivals, and openly so, but Eve still carries herself coolly, while Margo embarks upon a crisis of insecurity, self-doubt, alcohol abuse, and recriminations that only cease when Bill convinces her that he is in love only with her.

Though unsuccessful in replacing Margo in Bill's affections, Eve does in fact replace (or succeed) Margo in the theatre world and becomes the "new" Broadway sensation. Margo at long last makes a graceful exit, marries Bill, and moves on to the next stage in her life. As for Eve, she wins a prestigious award for her acting and gives a moving acceptance speech that endears her to everyone except those who know her well.

Following the awards ceremony, Eve returns home to find, waiting for her in the dark, a younger woman of humble appearance who eloquently professes her admiration for everything Eve is and does. Eve, susceptible as she is to such ardent displays of adoration, takes an interest in the girl and hires her as a personal assistant.

Double Mediation

Fortunately, the rivalry between Margo and Eve was short-lived because Margo realized that, though she could no longer have it all, she still had what mattered to her the most. In contrast, the legendary rivalry between actresses Bette Davis and Joan Crawford was in its third decade when *All About Eve* was filmed.

Significantly, Margo did not attempt to deprive Eve of anything that the latter had won from her. She made no attempt to spoil Eve's career, deciding instead to pass the mantle to her graciously by attending her award ceremony.

If Margo, driven by a desire for revenge, had attempted to sabotage Eve's budding career, we would have seen a case of what René Girard calls "double mediation." When *each* of the rivals is willing to destroy the object in order to deprive the other of it, the doubling is reciprocal. When only one of them does, the doubling is non-reciprocal. Both modes are pathological, for they draw the rivals toward neurosis and psychosis.

Margo was able to pull up out of a descent into madness. In the following story, one of the rivals also pulls back while the other is willing to destroy the coveted object rather than relinquish it to her.

NON-RECIPROCAL DOUBLING

When only one of two rivals loses sight of the original object in hisr passion to remove the other, the doubling is unidirectional, or non-reciprocal. The biblical story of Solomon's wisdom (1 Kings 3:16-28, NIV), illustrates this type of doubling:

> *Now two prostitutes came to the king and stood before him. One of them said, "Pardon me, my lord. This woman and I live in the same house, and I had a baby while she was there with me. The third day after my child was born, this woman also had a baby. We were alone; there was no one in the house but the two of us.*
>
> *"During the night this woman's son died because she lay on him. So she got up in the middle*

of the night and took my son from my side while I your servant was asleep. She put him by her breast and put her dead son by my breast. The next morning, I got up to nurse my son—and he was dead! But when I looked at him closely in the morning light, I saw that it wasn't the son I had borne."

The other woman said, "No! The living one is my son; the dead one is yours."

But the first one insisted, "No! The dead one is yours; the living one is mine." And so they argued before the king.

The king said, "This one says, 'My son is alive and your son is dead,' while that one says, 'No! Your son is dead and mine is alive.'"

Then the king said, "Bring me a sword." So they brought a sword for the king. He then gave an order: "Cut the living child in two and give half to one and half to the other."

The woman whose son was alive was deeply moved out of love for her son and said to the king, "Please, my lord, give her the living baby! Don't kill him!"

But the other said, "Neither I nor you shall have him. Cut him in two!"

Then the king gave his ruling: "Give the living baby to the first woman. Do not kill him; she is his mother."

When all Israel heard the verdict the king had given, they held the king in awe, because they saw that he had wisdom from God to administer justice.

Doubling occurs because the subject loses focus on the original object and objectifies the rival, treating himr as an impediment to be removed. The above story does not reveal whether both of the mothers initially lost focus on the infant, but clearly the real mother was the one who cared more about saving her child than about destroying her co-worker's happiness.

RECIPROCAL DOUBLING

When a rivalry becomes so intense that it threatens to turn mutually violent, it is a sign that the original object for which the rivals were competing has faded into insignificance beside two new objects—the rivals themselves, whose passion to destroy each other now takes precedence over all else. The concept of "mutual assured destruction" is illustrative: each of the two great powers competing for world domination would rather destroy the world than allow the other to dominate it.

This phenomenon finds cultural expression in traditions like warfare, duels to the death, and performative hand-to-hand combat sports like professional boxing. Such sports are better served by genuine rage than by tactics, because all that their audiences need for catharsis is to see two men viciously pounding each other until one of them is down.

SHOW NO MERCY

An infuriated driver who, coming upon a crowd of protesters, loses patience and plows through them has obviously prioritized one goal to the detriment of all others. That goal—e.g., to arrive before the train leaves, or to get home in time for a favorite TV program—has obscured and crowded out every other objective, even that of staying out of prison. Obscurity is total during this eclipse, for a medical and moral blackout has occurred—a failure of both consciousness and conscience. The only goal that matters to this driver is the one he has elevated above all others, and he is singularly focused on it to the point of dehumanizing anyone who stands in his way. Chief among the strong emotions that fuel his rampage is righteous rage, driven by the passionate conviction that he is an avenging angel dispensing God's own wrath. This is a momentary hallucination, for in truth he has demoted his god's own children to the status of road-kill.

In a similar scenario, a motorist plows through the protesters because he has been politically polarized to the extent that he sees them as less than human. This is how the politics of resentment bubbles up and finds expression in acts of violence.

"Show no mercy and take no prisoners!" orders the leader of the barbarian horde. Modern technology has enabled us to fire-bomb entire cities.

Strife Without Reason: The Duellists (1977)

The *Duellists*, a 1977 film directed by Ridley Scott and based on a story by Joseph Conrad, offers a superb example of non-reciprocal doubling. Conrad's story, in turn, is based on the true story of two hussars from different regiments in Napoleon's army.

When one of the hussars—Gabriel Ferraud (Harvey Keitel) kills the mayor of Strasbourg in a duel, the other—Armand d'Hubert (Keith Carradine) is sent to arrest him. He finds Ferraud at a rather formal musical salon hosted by a certain Mme de Lionne. A countertenor is performing, and Ferraud is standing just behind the elegant hostess reclining on her sofa. D'Hubert, quite impressive in his uniform, approaches her gallantly, kisses her hand, and asks to speak to Ferraud. When he takes Ferraud aside and delivers his message, Ferraud accuses him of humiliating him, demands immediate satisfaction, and attacks d'Hubert, forcing him to defend himself. The duel is inconclusive because Ferraud is wounded and cannot continue.

Though the two are in different regiments, their paths cross many times over the following 19 years. Each time they meet, Ferraud demands satisfaction, d'Hubert feels bound by their code of honor to duel with him, and, again, the duel ends when one of them is down and wounded. The historical record indicates that there were 30 duels.

The duels were fought with swords, sabers, and pistols, and in every case the entire ritual was conducted according to the 84 rules of dueling that had been set down during the French Renaissance in the 15th and 16th centuries. In the early 17th century, dueling was outlawed, but, late in the 18th, after the French Revolution, it was again allowed.

The 19th century was marked by turbulent fluctuations between Monarchist and Republican rule in France. In the century following the outbreak of the revolution in 1789, the country was a monarchy, then a republic, then an empire, then a monarchy again, then a republic again, then an empire again, and finally a republic. The duels between Ferraud and d'Hubert began during the first empire and ended sometime during the Bourbon Restoration of 1814–1830.

France's class system would never be eliminated but only reshaped in response to current socio-political ideologies. The bourgeoisie in France had always aped the desires of the aristocracy, but the very top-down hierarchical structure of society had precluded blatant imitations of aristocrats in certain matters of consumption such as clothing. From the late Middle Ages to the Revolution, sumptuary laws were enacted throughout France to restrain the conspicuous consumerism of the expanding bourgeoisie.

Mimetic theory predicts that conflict may arise if the subject seeks to appropriate the object of the model's desire. So, as the bourgeoisie became more prosperous over the centuries, the potential for conflict between the subject and the model-*cum*-obstacle-*cum*-rival increased.

Ferraud is from a lower social stratum than d'Hubert, who owns considerable property and has the manners of a gentleman. Ferraud is a social climber, as we discover when we first find him in the upper-class salon of Mme de Lionne, and his resentment of d'Hubert, who reeks of class in the noblest sense, is almost palpable.

In this species of triangle, the subject—more than ever fascinated by the model and imitating his desires—is nevertheless resentful that the objects of these desires are always held just beyond his reach. He imagines that the model himself is withholding them, and so he comes to regard his model as an obstacle. At that point, he has three options: (1) remove the obstacle, (2) continue resenting the obstacle, or (3) renounce his desire for it. Ferraud appears to believe that his festering boil of resentment can be lanced by killing its object.

REPOSITIONING OF THE OBJECT

When d'Hubert is asked what he and Ferraud are fighting about, he takes a puff on his pipe and replies, thoughtfully, "Only he knows." But we, at least, recognize that their first skirmish was prompted by Ferraud's loss of face before Mme de Lionne—a sudden narcissistic deflation that began when the dashing d'Hubert entered the salon and kissed her hand in greeting. Being arrested and conducted out of the salon further aggravated Ferraud's resentment of d'Hubert, and he interpreted the action as a deliberate affront to his honor. The people he had most hoped to impress had witnessed his humiliation before a rival, and his deflated image of himself could only be restored through an act of combat that would place him above that rival.

Mimetic theory confirms what we sense—that Ferraud would not have felt as threatened if d'Hubert had been of a lower social class and less dashing to boot. Ferraud's narcissism demanded that he find a suitable rival whom he could both admire and despise, for only by defeating such a rival could he recover his inflated image of himself as a matchless seducer and fierce warrior. A true warrior of the sort that had been modeled for him would never allow himself to be humiliated by a messenger bearing an arrest warrant.

As mimetic theory predicts, Ferraud loses sight of his object from the start. He is so obsessed with d'Hubert that he alternately accuses him of mentioning Mme de Lionne's name in public and not liking Napoleon Bonaparte. "What does Bonaparte have to do with this?" d'Hubert asks impatiently as he begins to realize that Ferraud is dangerously irrational. Shortly thereafter, when he calls Ferraud a "madman," Ferraud draws his sword and threatens to chase d'Hubert out of the *quartier* unless he agrees to fight. And so begins their 19-year-long succession of duels—a microcosm of the Napoleonic wars that were going on at the time.

Years later, d'Hubert's reflection on Ferraud's motivation (i.e., that only Ferraud knows why they are fighting) is a clear and succinct statement of the story's theme. *The Duellists* is not about dueling. Nor is it about the Napoleonic wars. And there are better viewing options if all one wants to see is a good guy defeating a bad one.

Central to the story's theme is the disappearance of the object from its usual corner of the mimetic triangle. Neither of the adversaries can accurately identify what they're fighting about. After the 1814 Bourbon Restoration, Ferraud can no longer accuse

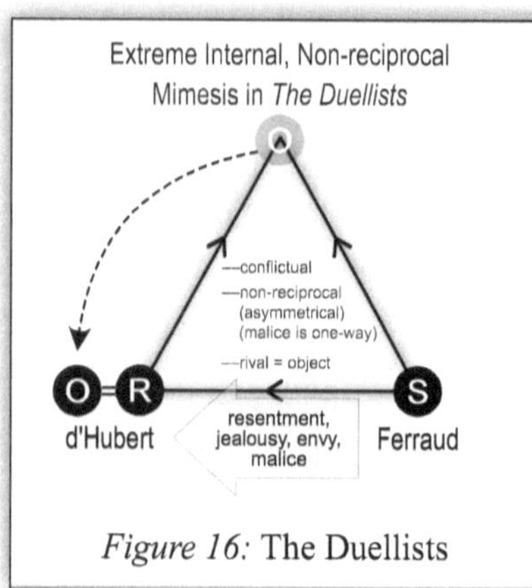

Figure 16: The Duellists

d'Hubert of disliking Bonaparte, but that doesn't end the dueling.

D'Hubert doesn't know what the object is because his desires are not mediated (modeled for him) by Ferraud. Ferraud doesn't know because he has unconsciously refocused his desires on d'Hubert. What he wants is what d'Hubert already has—status, charm, respect, breeding, good looks, etc.—but he simultaneously sees d'Hubert as an obstacle because d'Hubert is the current proprietor of these qualities. Ferraud's malice toward d'Hubert is born out of his denial of his real desire, which is to fill his own emptiness by appropriating the being of another man.

There are, for Ferraud, two d'Huberts—one a metaphysical object and one a model-turned-obstacle, and Ferraud imagines he can appropriate the former by eliminating the latter. This is of course delusional, for killing d'Hubert will never result in his appropriating d'Hubert's essence,

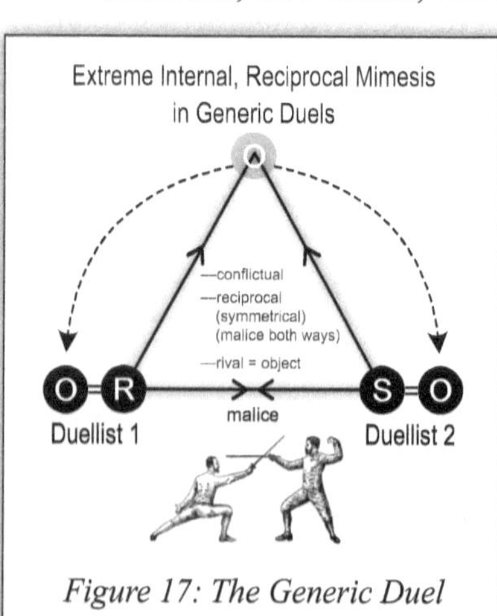

Figure 17: The Generic Duel

though doing so might momentarily re-inflate Ferraud's narcissism.

Ferraud's desires are "metaphysical"—i.e., a mirage—insofar as their objects are abstract entities such as breeding, charm, and social status—all of which amount to d'Hubert's very being and substance. Ferraud feels deprived of these qualities and certain that his lack of them cannot be his fault. He must find someone else to blame. What better candidate than the man who, already possessing those qualities and having modeled them for him, now comes to withhold them and push him down even farther in the society that he aspires to be a part of.

Though d'Hubert seems to intuit some of the dynamics of this conflict, Ferraud seems completely unconscious of them. They account for his paranoia, as d'Hubert appears to him as the primary agent of what he regards as his persecution.

Figure 17 represents a more typical, or "generic" duel in which the adversaries are in a reciprocal relation-ship marked by symmetrical desire and malice. They are attempting to restore a hierarchical difference that has been lost in the mimetic feedback loop of their rivalry.

In psychoanalysis, a double is one whose presence has the awesome power to both inflate and deflate the subject's narcissistic projections of himself. The narcissist's self-image rests precariously on the double's perception of him. The double may initially appear godlike, but he becomes a devil if he obstructs the very desires that he has modeled for the subject. The narcissistic subject is always vulnerable to slights because they bring into consciousness his own nullity— his sensed impoverishment of being—as well as his mortality. In primitive animism, the double manifests as a reflection, a twin, a portrait, or a shadow who may either guarantee immortality or foreshadow death.

In the film, the fortune-teller who describes their duels as "strife without reason," and "a quarrel pursued for its own sake" is only reflecting on the uncanny nature of the duel, but she would be mistaken to conclude that Ferraud has no real personal reason to continue challenging d'Hubert. She just doesn't understand what that reason is any more than he does.

A final word must be said about d'Hubert, whose desires seem to be of a completely different order than Ferraud's. In order to fight Ferraud, he must desire to defeat him, but he is very clear that he does not wish to kill him. In fact, he appears to have no complaint against Ferraud and even once intercedes for him when he is being disciplined by his superiors.

In short, d'Hubert fights Ferraud while feeling no malice toward him. This is what makes their contests non-reciprocal.

In that case, what *does* motivate d'Hubert to fight? What is the object of *his* desire in this triangle? The film does not interrogate him on these matters, but we may infer that he is meant to represent an outstanding officer in every way—a model for others, in fact. Ferraud evidently sees him in this way. This would lead us to believe that d'Hubert's own mediated desire is to continue being what he already is, and so he behaves accordingly, conscientiously performing the required rituals of warfare and honorable conduct.

The Picture of Dorian Gray

Oscar Wilde's Gothic novel, *The Picture of Dorian Gray* (1890) is about a man who trades his soul for the chance to satisfy two mediated but incompatible desires.

Dorian's stately and alluring beauty inspires the artist Basil Hallward to paint his portrait. In a conversation with his friend, Lord Henry Wotton, Basil confesses that he worships Dorian:

> *Of course I flatter him dreadfully. I find a strange pleasure in saying things to him that I know I shall be sorry for having said. As a rule, he is charming to me, and we sit in the studio and talk of a thousand things. Now and then, however, he is horribly thoughtless, and seems to take a real delight in giving me pain. Then I feel, Harry, that I have given away my whole soul to some one who treats it as if it were a flower to put in his coat, a bit of decoration to charm his vanity, an ornament for a summer's day.*
>
> Wilde, Oscar. *The Picture of Dorian Gray* (Dover Thrift Editions). Dover Publications. Kindle Edition.

The painter's fascination with the object of his gaze becomes Dorian's own, for what Dorian sees in the portrait is his own image as reflected in the eyes of a highly sensitive and appreciative admirer. Basil, purposefully or not, has modeled his desire, and Dorian is mimetically "learning" to worship himself as Basil does.

When Lord Henry hears Basil's impassioned descriptions of Dorian, he, too, becomes fascinated with Dorian, though he has not yet met him. Soon after they do meet, he surpasses Basil's flattery with some of his own, further priming Dorian's narcissism and drawing him into a mimetic relation of mentor-to-mentee.

Lord Henry desires a life devoted entirely to the pursuit of beauty and sensual pleasure and the denial of death and decay. The following passage from Chapter 2 is worth quoting:

> *(To Dorian) If you stay any longer in this glare you will be quite spoiled, and Basil will never paint*

you again. You really must not allow yourself to become sunburnt. It would be unbecoming."

"What can it matter?" cried Dorian Gray, laughing, as he sat down on the seat at the end of the garden.

"It should matter everything to you, Mr. Gray."

"Why?"

"Because you have the most marvelous youth, and youth is the one thing worth having."

"I don't feel that, Lord Henry."

"No, you don't feel it now. Some day, when you are old and wrinkled and ugly, when thought has seared your forehead with its lines, and passion branded your lips with its hideous fires, you will feel it, you will feel it terribly. Now, wherever you go, you charm the world. Will it always be so? ... You have a wonderfully beautiful face, Mr. Gray. Don't frown. You have. And Beauty is a form of Genius—is higher, indeed, than Genius, as it needs no explanation. It is of the great facts of the world, like sunlight, or spring-time, or the reflection in dark waters of that silver shell we call the moon. It cannot be questioned. It has its divine right of sovereignty. It makes princes of those who have it.

You smile? Ah! when you have lost it you won't smile.... People say sometimes that Beauty is only superficial. That may be so. But at least it is not so superficial as Thought is. To me, Beauty is the wonder of wonders. It is only shallow people who do not judge by appearances. The true mystery of the world is the visible, not the invisible.... Yes, Mr. Gray, the gods have been good to you. But what the gods give they quickly take away. You have only a few years in which to live really, perfectly, and fully. When your youth goes, your beauty will go with it, and then you will suddenly discover that there are no triumphs left for you, or have to content yourself with those mean triumphs that the memory of your past will make more bitter than defeats. Every month as it wanes brings you nearer to something dreadful. Time is jealous of you, and wars against your lilies and your roses. You will become sallow, and hollow-cheeked, and dull-eyed. You will suffer horribly.... Ah! realize your youth while you have it. Don't squander the gold of your days, listening to the tedious, trying to improve the hopeless failure, or giving away your life to the ignorant, the common, and the vulgar. These are the sickly aims, the false ideals, of our age. Live! Live the wonderful life that is in you! Let nothing be lost upon you. Be always searching for new sensations. Be afraid of nothing.... A new Hedonism—that is what our century wants. You might be its visible symbol. With your personality there is nothing you could not do. The world belongs to you for a season....

The moment I met you I saw that you were quite unconscious of what you really are, of what you really might be. There was so much in you that charmed me that I felt I must tell you something about yourself. I thought how tragic it would be if you were wasted. For there is such a little time that your youth will last—such a little time. The common hill-flowers wither, but they blossom again. The laburnum will be as yellow next June as it is now. In a month there will be purple stars on the clematis, and year after year the green night of its leaves will hold its purple stars. But we never get back our youth. The pulse of joy that beats in us at twenty, becomes sluggish. Our limbs fail, our senses rot. We degenerate into hideous puppets, haunted by the memory of the passions of which we were too much afraid, and the exquisite temptations that we had not the courage to yield to. Youth! Youth! There is absolutely nothing in the world but youth!"

These opinions make quite an impression on Dorian, whose narcissism has already been overinflated by Basil's flattery.

Like Narcissus gazing into the pool, Dorian worships the image captured in his reflection, and now he yearns to possess it in perpetuity for his own embodied self. Possessing the portrait itself will not help. He must appropriate its unchanging beauty.

But he cannot possess both objects of his desire, for they are incompatible. Hedonistic pursuits will hasten and even worsen the fading of his beauty. This is something Lord Henry does not mention to him, instead urging him to "always be searching for new sensations" and to become the "visible symbol of a new Hedonism."

Faced with these two compelling but incompatible desires and unwilling to accept the transitory nature of his physical beauty any more than does Lord Henry, Dorian fervently wishes to switch places with the portrait. The portrait's durable beauty will transfer to him, while the consequences of his libertine lifestyle will be visible only in the painted image, which he will sequester.

His wish is mysteriously granted—perhaps by Lord Henry himself, who represents the Tempter, considering what follows. After callously driving an actress of his acquaintance to suicide, Dorian notices a slight shift in the eyes of his portrait double: they now appear somewhat cruel.

Dorian continues his debauchery for many years without showing any signs of aging or wear. He looks as handsome and stately as his portrait image once did. The portrait image, however, has become hideous.

The rest of Dorian Gray's story is well-known and contains more rich veins of insight about mimetic desire than I can tap into in this short volume. René Girard, who elaborated mimetic theory decades before mirror neurons were discovered, always maintained that great literature is the gateway to the inner sanctum of the human drama and that it can reveal things that are hidden in most narratives—things hidden "since the foundation of the world," as he puts it. (*Des choses cachées depuis la fondation du monde,* Grasset, 1978)

The Chosen One

His father grooms him to inherit the family business and has high expectations of him. The elder Trump models his M.O. as well as his dubious values system for young Donald, who is eager to mimic them and then does so all his life.

In their triangle, the object of the son's desires are copies of everything that the father desires—wealth, power, and fame—all of which serve the two men's narcissistic inflations. When these projections are cast upon the big screen of celebrity, the stakes can be very high, for the opposite of monumental success is monumental failure.

His father teaches him the importance of image in a world where all that matters is how conspicuously wealthy you can be and whom you know. Donald adopts a value system that divides people into two categories— winners and losers, and he knows he must not fail, for his father has taught him that no one is more contemptible than a loser. By this time, the obsessive self-image formation has already produced an heightened level of doubling, because Donald Jr.'s self-esteem is now firmly anchored to an image that he ardently desires to see reflected in other people's eyes but knows he cannot always control. He is awed and terrified by the power of that reflected image to affect his moods (which, as we've shown, are shaped and triggered by the interdividual rapport and the self-image that it engenders), and he swings from narcissistic inflation to deflation, depending on his ability to surround himself with loyal admirers and to dismiss or bully anyone who becomes an obstacle. He *needs* to believe the cheering crowd is larger than it actually is and that he's the greatest president ever.

Ferraud the duelist has a singular double, but Donald has a multiplicity of them—not just individuals but entire institutions and classes of people. Identifying his *double du jour* is just a matter of listening to his daily rants.

Much like Ferraud's double, Donald's are both gods and demons. To understand why this is so, consider first of all that the reputation of New York City realtors has long been tainted by its association with the Five Families (of organized crime). Then consider that NYC is a big city with an incredible diversity of people trying to figure out how to live with each other and sorting themselves out 24-7. Social hierarchies are constantly shifting among the winners and the losers. And finally, consider that New York's elites have never believed the Trumps had any "class."

They won't let him into their clubs, so he builds several of his own, but even that does not temper his resentment of the elites. It just raises the stakes.

Thus, Donald's malice toward the elites is born out of his resentment toward people better educated than himself, more "cultured," and held in higher esteem. He wants what they have, but they look down on him because of his shady dealings, his coarseness, and his moral defects, which he carries like a chip on his shoulder. This kind of obsessive malice was Ferraud's problem as well, and it all began with envy.

If, in each case, the double is the model-turned-obstacle, it is because neither Donald nor Ferraud realizes at any time that what he really desires will never be his, for it is a plenitude of being that he imagines can only belong to others and that can therefore not be bought. But he persists in believing that it can be.

The double is both oneself and the other. The subject gazes at the other—the double—and sees his own reflection. He alternately sees himself and the double in rapid succession until the two begin to merge and he becomes convinced that they are the same and must be separated. But must they be separated? And can they be?

The subject wants separation from the double-as-rival but will never have it as long as he is obsessed with possessing the rival's being. He believes the double is holding him hostage, but the reverse is true. This is the "aggrieved" persecutor who hallucinates that he is in fact the victim. It is the repudiated narcissist lashing out at those who do not worship him.

Donald tries to rid himself of the evil double by cultivating an ally of comparable mass and influence, and for Donald, that is a political party that he can marshal around his ego for protection from his "persecutors."

Image is everything to Donald. His self-esteem depends utterly on it. This is why he cannot allow criticism of any kind and surrounds himself with sycophants and worshippers who will praise him for becoming all that his father and Roy Cohn expected him to be—ruthless in his quest for money, power, and fame, unwilling to accept defeat at any price, and contemptuous of the law.

His worship of Mammon is ancillary to his worship of the inflated image that his admirers and vanquished enemies project back to him. His fear of his home newspaper (*The New York Times*) is ancillary to his fear of his own deflated image.

THE HALLUCINATORY PHASE

These patterns of doubling are not unique to Donald. They are observed wherever conditions are conducive to mimesis and rivalry, from the Mafia to the White House and from the corporate boardroom to sporting events. It's only when they enter the hallucinatory phase that they begin to be recognized by those still capable of distinguishing the hallucinatory from the real.

In Donald's case, a further distinction must be made between hallucination and conscious political strategy. Roy Cohn's mentorship of Donald in the 1970s and 1980s suggests the latter, but Donald's characterizations of people and events have often suggested some kind of hallucinatory disturbance. Whatever accounts for these aberrations, they have been faithfully mimicked by his followers—the multitudinous "subjects" to his "model."

Shared delusions and hallucinations—both mimetic phenomena—are popularly known as *folies à deux* when two people share them, but francophones can replace *deux* with other numbers or just describe the disorders as *folies en famille*. Clinically, these shared *folies* are jointly known as delusional disorders, and there is no limit to the number of people who can share them, whether or not they are induced and orchestrated by a dominant, charismatic figure like Trump. This is modeling for the multitudes. Where shared delusions or hallucinations are *not* induced, they are usually limited to two already psychotically disordered individuals who mimetically trigger each other's distorted perceptions.

Mass Delusions

We know that one person's hallucination can mimetically induce millions of copies of itself, and that appears to happen wherever Trump's followers are unable to make the all-important distinction between fantasy and reality. Many others, mimicking Donald's political machinations, don't care whether the hallucinations are real or contrived as long as they serve their purpose. Irrational fears, paranoia, and conspiracy theories are the authoritarian's tools of the trade.

The doubling that I have described was Donald's overarching one, but there were others. Trump, like Cohn, wanted to prove he was man who could get away with anything, so anything that thwarted that desire became his double. Looked at broadly, that obstacle/double was the law itself and, by extension, all people and institutions that tried to subject him to the law—the courts, the media, Democrats, public opinion, scientists, a branch of Congress, and innumerable others.

The consequences of these patterns of doubling, as exhibited by the Trump phenomenon, were catastrophic. The events around January 6 left a very broad-based impression that the insurgents were severely out of touch with reality.

Our only consolation may be that the entire Trump phenomenon has been exceedingly well documented since its beginnings and will therefore be of inestimable value to students of abnormal psychology, mass delusions, and totalitarian forms of government.

Limping Through Life

The 1934 Hollywood version of Somerset Maugham's partly autobiographical 1915 novel, *Of Human Bondage*, stars Leslie Howard as Philip Carey, a

mediocre art student whose output consists mainly of female nudes. Told by his mentor that he has little talent, he abandons art and enters medical school in London.

Philip has a club foot and is easily embarrassed by it. It undermines his confidence, especially in the pursuit of love, but like Cyrano de Bergérac, he is gifted with words. His friend and fellow medical student, Cyril, is tongue-tied around women and cannot easily flirt, but he imagines that Philip must have considerable experience with women for having lived in Paris and painted them. So he asks Philip to accompany him to a tea room where a pretty waitress has captured his attention. Philip is to show him how to woo her.

Maugham himself was a stutterer, and he was also three-quarters homosexual—as he estimated in his later years. These irregularities set him apart from other men and made him self-conscious and ill-at-ease around them. Philip's club foot serves as a fitting symbol of Maugham's problematic sexual responses, and Cyril's difficulties expressing himself reflect Maugham's own.

At the tea room, Philip and Cyril observe the waitress (Mildred, played by Bette Davis) flirting with a loutish salesman (Emil) at a nearby table. Cyril seems smitten with her and looks to Philip for affirmation that she is desirable. But Philip is unimpressed, dismissing her as "an anemic little waitress." He summons her to their table and flirts with her in an ungentlemanly way, even asking personal questions and commenting on her pelvis in a mock-doctorly way. She responds with icy indifference, tells Philip she had thought he was a gentleman, then storms away in a huff. Cyril now confesses that he was wrong about her and apologizes to Philip for bringing him to meet her, saying that she is "ill-natured and contemptible." His opinion of her has now been shaped by Philip's.

It is hard to know how audiences of the 1930s interpreted that scene, but "woke" audiences of the 21st century would probably agree with Mildred's assessment of Philip rather than Cyril's assessment of Mildred. While Philip is distinctly upper-class, Mildred's Cockney accent and obvious lack of what he regards as good breeding make her an easy target for his disrespectful teasing. These differences, added to the general impression that she is a woman of dubious character and he an educated and temperate man of means, are patently meant to prejudice us against her from the start, for she is to be the *functional* scapegoat of the story—a role that will become clearer in Chapter 4 of this book, "Representations."

Cyril leaves the tea room and Philip stays behind. Alone at his table, he appears to reconsider his earlier judgment of her. He calls her over again and turns on the charm, this time getting her to crack a smile and agree to meet him later at Victoria Station. But why? What happened in those few moments to excite his interest in her, despite her haughty indifference toward him?

Mimetic theory offers several ways of understanding this, all of which can be represented as triangles of desire.

First of all, Philip's emergent desire has been modeled for him by two men—Cyril and the salesman, Emil Miller. The former has modeled more serious intentions toward Mildred than has the latter, and Philip's intentions appear to fall somewhere between.

The irony is that Cyril and Philip are looking to each other for mentorship in the arts of love, but only Philip knows that he has little wisdom to impart. Neither of them knows what to desire and must imitate the other's perceived desire. Philip is simply the cleverer of the two, for he artfully redirects Cyril's desire away from Mildred once Cyril has designated her as a desirable object. Elimination of the rival is the first step toward possession of the object.

Philip is afraid of getting what he now wants, for he has experienced the thrill of a burgeoning desire that must not be satisfied lest it wane. But desire can only thrive in the presence of a rival, or obstacle. Now that Cyril is out of the picture, Philip needs a new obstacle to recharge his desire. Having sized Mildred up in his initial "interview" with her, he concludes that she herself is the perfect candidate.

They begin a long and painful relationship during which she coldly rebuffs him at almost every turn, leaving him feeling frustrated but even more desirous than ever. When she does agree to meet him, it's with a shrug and a haughty "I don't mind," as if she's just doing him a favor. He offers to marry her, but she refuses. She will always scorn him as long as she thinks she has a better offer. He daydreams about her constantly, even during his medical-school exam, which he therefore fails.

Mildred is a saucy Cockney trapped in a triangle of her own. What she lacks and very much desires is class. But Britain's rigid class structure rules out social mobility, and thus she sees the upper classes as obstacles to that desire. While resenting their indifference toward her, she also mimics it in every encounter with Philip. She puts on grand airs. She will not allow him to feel superior to her and continually puts him down, playing on his insecurities about his club foot and running off with other men. The first of these is Emil the salesman, who gets her pregnant and then dumps her. She returns to Philip and, with mock contrition, asks if he still wants to marry her. He seems unsure, for his desire for her has waned, but he declares that he still loves her in spite of himself. He sets her up in a flat and buys her pretty dresses.

As soon as the baby is born, she wastes no time finding an off-site nursemaid to relieve her of the burdens of motherhood.

At this point, Philip may marry Mildred if he so wishes, but his desire again needs a rival. So he invites his lecherous friend Harry to come to a tea room with them. When he arrives and Mildred asks him why he didn't bring his girl, he laughs loudly and says, "I'm not interested in *my* girls. I'm only interested in *other men's* girls!" His intentions are thus made abundantly clear to Philip if not to Mildred. Harry and Mildred have a great time, drinking, laughing, and flirting, all the while ignoring Philip, who is left to pay the tab.

The following day, Philip rebukes Mildred for her behavior at the tea room, and she announces that she and Harry love each other and are going to Paris. Philip is crushed and lashes out her, calling her cheap and vulgar.

After her fling with Harry, she returns to London, destitute. Harry has the constables remove her from his doorstep. Once again, she returns to Philip, who gives her and the baby a spare room in his flat. Mildred, now showing signs of wear, pretends to have had a change of heart about Philip and reminds him of his much-earlier offer of marriage. His expression shows that he doubts her sincerity, and he responds with the same indifference that she once showed toward him. His attention is in fact divided between her and a small pile of travel brochures lying nearby. The movement of desire has reversed itself, and when she attempts to seduce him, he rebuffs her, saying, "You disgust me."

Mildred flies into a rage and delivers a tirade on the theme of *her* disgust toward *him*, a "cripple." After he leaves, she goes on a rampage of destruction, burning some bonds that his uncle gave him to pay for his re-entry into medical school, ripping up his medical books, trashing his flat, and slashing his beloved paintings.

Philip's money is gone and he is forced to leave medical school. But before he does, the chief surgeon at the hospital offers to do something about his foot. The surgery is successful and Philip can now walk all over London looking for employment. Unsuccessful in finding any, he returns to his flat to find that his landlady has locked him out for nonpayment of rent. Exhausted and discouraged, he visits a man named Athelny, a former patient who had taken an interest in him and frequently invited him for dinner, where his lovely daughter, Sally, has also taken an interest in him.

Seeing Philip's condition and learning of his eviction, Athelny insists that Philip stay with him and Sally until his prospects improve, and he offers Philip a job in his department store.

Philip seems quite happy working there, but he receives a notice that his uncle has died, leaving him a small fortune. At last, he can return to medical school.

Some time later, shortly after graduating, he is accepted for a position as ship's doctor on a cruise ship that will take him away for two years. Sally's tears prompt a conversation between them about their feelings for each other, and Philip asks her to marry him upon his return. She consents without hesitation but on condition that he still wants her then. She is staking no claim on him.

Philip is informed that Mildred is hospitalized. He finds her looking wasted, and a cursory examination reveals that she has tuberculosis (originally syphilis, in the book). He asks about the baby, and she replies, "Dead." She begs his forgiveness for having treated him so awfully and tells him he is, after all, a gentleman. Doubting her sincerity once again, he is unmoved.

Philip has been having a reckoning with himself during the years that have separated them, and seeing her this one last time has triggered a process of recognition. Philip realizes that he has been "limping through life," and that the time has come to find his footing in it.

Sally is waiting for him on the steps outside the hospital. He announces that he's not taking the job on the cruise ship, tears up the travel brochures, throws them on the sidewalk, and asks her to marry him without further delay.

LA RONDE DE L'AMOUR

Norah cares for Philip, Philip cares only for Mildred, and Mildred gives herself to a succession of men who do not care for her. In Maugham's novel, as in life, sexual appetite and love are always complicated by mediated desire. In Philip's case, the mediation must be internal—which is to say, conflictual. There must be a rival to obstruct his desire so that he can experience it in its pure and unrequited form. But, while other men might allow the rivalry to escalate, Philip only watches as Harry seduces Mildred in front of his very eyes. Harry's comment about being interested "only in other men's girls" suggests that Philip has manipulated him. Here, the manipulation consists of modeling his own desire (as the current owner of the object) for Harry to imitate, because Harry can only desire what other men already possess.

Philip is involved with two sets of people in this drama—those who are deeply mired in these dynamics of mediated desire (Cyril, Emil, and Harry) and those who appear not to be (Norah and Sally). Philip's nascent understanding of these dynamics shows him a path toward something of greater value than desire itself.

Groucho Marx famously said, "I don't want to be a member of any club that would have me as a member." For a while, Philip couldn't love anyone who loved him and loved only the one who couldn't return his love.

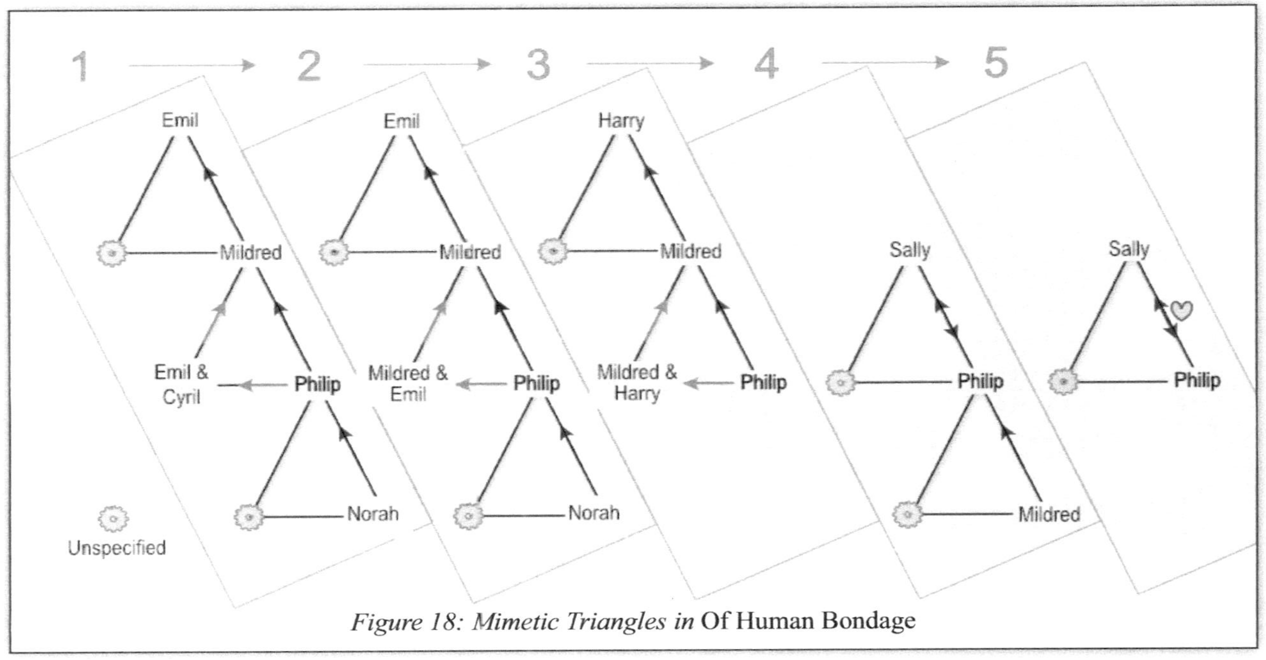

Figure 18: Mimetic Triangles in Of Human Bondage

83

Chapter 3: Scapegoating

Misrecognition

Our historically recent but now commonplace understanding of scapegoating is that it singles out individuals or minority groups for persecution. But we often disagree about which individuals or groups are practicing it and which are its victims. After centuries of slavery in the US, significant numbers of white American males are not only minimizing or dismissing that history but claiming victim status for themselves vis-à-vis Blacks. Even the most egregious persecutors never seem to recognize themselves as such and may even be proud of what they've done. Misrecognition is the *sine qua non* of the act.

Denial vs. Recognition of Guilt

Those engaged in acts of persecution do not see themselves as persecutors—the word itself would imply that their victims are innocent—but rather as avengers sent from the sovereign God, state, emperor, or proletariat. As the smoke begins to clear and their vengeance is spent, their first impulse may be to recoil from the damage they have done, but the impulse to either deny or justify it usually follows close behind. Contrition requires a level of recognition that is rare.

Here are a few of the many ways in which cruelties are rationalized:

- Denial:
  - *The Holocaust never happened.*
  - *The American Civil War was about states' rights, not slavery.*
- Dehumanization of the victim:
  - *They were parasites / vermin / scum / savages / an inferior race.*
- Silencing and/or erasure
  - *We shall not speak of ...*
    ... the massacres of native Americans.
    ... the Prince's assassination of Jamal Khashoggi.
    ... your father's participation in the ...
        ... KKK
        ... Nazi party.
        ... US Capitol riot.
  - *The authorities have no record of any such person/ event.*
  - *"There are no homosexuals in Iran."*
    (Iranian President Ahmadinejad in 2007)

- Intimidation:
  - *Who you gonna believe–me, or your own eyes?*
- Settling scores (tit for tat).
  - *He was a child molester.*
  - *He killed my lover.*
- Revisionism:
  - *Some of them [the Capitol insurrectionists of 1/6/21] went in, and they're hugging and kissing the police and the guards, you know? They had great relationships."*
    (Donald Trump to Fox News host Laura Ingraham)

- Blame-shifting to the victim:
  - *She made me do it to her. (rape, assault)*
  - *She was asking for it. (ditto)*
  - *He passed a counterfeit 20-dollar bill.* (and for that I had my knee on his neck for more than nine minutes.)
  - *He cut me off. (road rage)*

- Appeal to scripture or patriotism.
  - *They were an abomination in the eyes of God.*
  - *Mike Pence is a traitor.*

Sin, guilt, debit, debt, and fault

"Debt is just another word for guilt," says a headline in the *Financial Times*. We know from historical and comparative linguistics that the concepts of guilt, debt, and debits are related. In the Germanic languages, the concepts of debt and guilt are conveyed by a single term: *Schuld* (variously *skuld*, etc.). The German *Entschuldigen Sie, bitte* translates into English as "Excuse me, please"—a modest request for assistance. But at a more literal level, linguistically, it is an invitation to debit the requester in return for some small favor.

The Latin expression *Mea culpa* means "the fault is mine." In English, the verb "inculpate" means to assign guilt. *Culpa* comes into Italian as *colpa* and into Spanish as *culpa*. The French word for "guilty" is the derivative *coupable*. The English word "sin" is thought to be from the Latin *sons*, meaning "guilt," and the word "guilt" is from Old English *gylt*, which may be translated as "sin" or "fault."

Sin, guilt, debit, debt, and fault. All are the universal functions of any society managing conflict. All may be ritualistically transferred to some individual or group specially chosen for the task of removing them. Purification is the end product of this process.

Blame, accusations, and calumnies are the preferred instruments of this process, which can only succeed when a certain critical mass of individuals can agree on the guilt of the victim(s). As we shall see, such an agreement always involves a polarization of animus in which the collectivity stops infighting and focuses its aggressions on the victim(s).

Guilt Shifting

The process of guilt shifting that culminates in scapegoating is driven by tensions within a community that is stressed by disease, internal strife, or other existential threats. The community must act decisively to restore order but cannot identify the real causes of its troubles. Grudges, suspicions, and accusations are rife. Adversaries cast derogatory and dehumanizing epithets at each other (cows, dogs, pigs, rats, hyenas, parasites, and the like) in order to deflect blame from themselves, for they know, or believe, that their troubles will not end until the "guilty" party—the troublemaker—is identified and either killed or expelled.

People whose problem-solving faculties have been shaped by modern science will recognize that neither the plague nor HIV nor COVID-19 was the work of malign individuals or groups. They may also recognize the sacrificial nature of slanders against those wrongly accused of deliberately spreading such diseases. Ignorance, selfishness, or carelessness may rightfully be blamed for their spread, but human sacrifice is hardly a fitting remedy for those faults. Nor is dehumanization. Education and rehabilitation are surer ways of containing and remedying the damage and preventing its recurrence while ensuring that as many people as possible are held within the purview of the law.

Pre-modern societies, even extant ones, are ill-equipped to adopt such pragmatic approaches. They are confronted with a state of affairs that appears unsustainable and, if left unchecked, will escalate into ethnocide—the violence of all against all. No society can allow this to happen.

What follows, then, is a spontaneous and unconscious polarization of all animus, leading to the violence of all against one—a lynching, for example. Simply put, one individual is blamed for everything and ritually sacrificed or expelled. The community is purged of its troubles through a process that circumvents recognition of itself. That process is non-conscious and highly specific. To be effective, it *must not* be brought into consciousness. Like a precious potion, the truth—i. e., that a ritualized murder has occurred—must be carefully contained so that it neither spills nor leaks. As we hope to show, this is the genesis of the Sacred—a cover-up for a lynching.

Paleolithic and Neolithic tribes caught up in the victimary process, whether spontaneously or ritually, could not have seen their chosen targets as innocent victims because the concepts of scapegoating and victimage did not yet exist. But we are privileged to see that about them. We recognize specious reasoning used to assign blame. We question divine mandates and rushes to judgment. In short, we can and do ask questions about what happened because we are not under the spell of the sacred that once prohibited those questions.

The *concept* of scapegoating arises only when the sacrificial act is finally recognized as irrational, hallucinatory, and murderous. Only then does an inversion occur in which the community's role is recognized by outsiders and/or later generations as persecutory. Until the early modern era, such recognitions were extremely rare. Even now, individuals or crowds engaged in persecutory behavior virtually never recognize it as scapegoating, though outsiders and later generations are more likely to do so.

A classic example of this phenomenon is the Third Reich's treatment of Jews during the Nazi era. What was obvious to the rest of the world as well as later generations of Germans was strangely veiled so that the German public could not see it for what it was. Psychologists and neuroscientists are interested in how such veils are formed and why.

At what point the epithet becomes a hallucination and the metaphor shapes reality is not always clear, but Nazi propaganda characterizing Jews as "parasites" led to their extermination using a pesticide (Zyklon B) previously used to kill lice.

IMAGES MATTER.

Our images, as perceived by others as well as ourselves, are imprinted on the currency of guilt and innocence that we all exchange and carry with us. They are woven from stories and anecdotes, memoirs, attack ads, the face in the bathroom mirror, portraits, photos, social messaging, and virtually everything else that objectifies us. We experience ourselves as both subjects and objects, as demonstrated by the first three words in this very sentence, where the verb "experience" is used reflexively because its subject and its object are the same. It is in this sense that our "ego" is at every moment a more or less fluid amalgam of images reflected back to us, past and present, and constantly sorting themselves out in our unconscious.

Guilt and the Specter of Social Death

Fears of exclusion motivate patterns of denial and deflection of guilt. Guilt is a social debit. An accumulation of guilt threatens to make one an object rather than a subject of political power. Extreme accumulation presages an exclusion by the sovereign juridical or administrative order into a zone of what Giorgio Agamben has called "bare life," i.e., a life outside the domain of law and without its protections, but, paradoxically, still under its jurisdiction.

The concept of "social death" is integral to any study of the human sciences. Our fears of it sometimes overshadow our fears of actual death, as many combat veterans have reported. In primitive societies, expulsion or abandonment by one's community is, practically speaking, a death warrant. In modern societies, such an expulsion is perhaps no less traumatizing, but migration to another community is more often an available option.

A POLYTHEISTIC MODEL OF SOCIAL DEATH

Agamben cites a juridical classification from ancient Roman law—that of the *homo sacer* (sacred man), defined as one who may be killed but must not be sacrificed. Since every known system of law includes a prohibition against murder, the legal-and-yet-illegal "killing" of a *homo sacer* is made possible by an exception declared by the sovereign power. In our world, the *state of exception* is often expressed as a state of emergency, wherein the sovereign power suspends its own laws in order to transgress them with impunity. The US's post-9/11 detention of suspected terrorists without trial in an offshore prison facility at Guantánamo Bay, Cuba, is but one recent instance of the state of exception. The 1991 invasion of Iraq is another.

Just as there is no law against killing animals, there's no law against killing the *homo sacer*. Sovereign power is the power to separate the domain of citizens (political beings) from that of mere bodies.

In Roman law, the *homo sacer* was typically one who had violated an oath to Jupiter, the divine lawmaker responsible for social order. The oath-taker ceremonially invited punishment by Jupiter if he did not fulfill his oath. If he did break his oath, he became the property of

Orcus, the god of broken oaths and the lord of the underworld.

But the oath-breaker was not to be *sacrificed*, for doing so would pre-empt Orcus's custody over him and re-introduce him into the political and religious order from which he had been excluded.

As I write, a majority of US states are attempting to circumvent constitutional law in order to suppress voting by non-whites, thus excluding them from political life and reducing them, once again, to "bare life," the life of the slave, the prison inmate, and the unfortunate individual who is caught driving while Black. The "bare life" is also the life of excluded groups—European Jews, Native Americans, the Rohingya of Myanmar, and countless others who have been treated as mere bodies by the state.

If we view this internal/external opposition in terms of generality/exception, we observe that neither would be possible without the other. A generality presupposes a hypothetical or real exception, and vice versa. Similarly, the domain of law could not exist without a domain outside it. Paradoxically, the former also encompasses the latter and sets its boundaries. This is the privilege and the peril of sovereignty.

The tendency of democratic systems of governance is to ensure that no one is a mere body and that everyone is guaranteed political power by law. The apportionment of power then becomes the salient issue for competing interests, and a strong juridical system is needed to keep the peace between them. Majorities are less likely to oppress minorities if everyone's rights are enshrined in a sovereign constitution.

At the other end of the scale, totalitarian systems invest all power in a single individual or presidium. This is the power to have political enemies eliminated and to move bodies around at will. In totalitarian states, the juridical system is a sham. The leader's (or leaders') will is supreme.

A MONOTHEISTIC MODEL

The monotheistic world of Judaeo-Christianity worked on a slightly different model than the Roman one but accomplished the same ends—expulsion, purification, and the strengthening of the social order. It was the One Sovereign God who created the state of exception whereby the general rules regarding murder or other forms of cruelty were suspended. Thus, the divine prohibition against murder did not save the Canaanites from slaughter by the Israelites following their exodus from Egypt.

> *And they utterly destroyed all that was in the city, both man and woman, young and old, ox and sheep and donkey, with the edge of the sword.*
>
> (Joshua 6:21)

Modern warfare has demonstrated its capacity for barbarity at an even grander scale. A nation that calls itself "Christian" is no less capable than the ancient Israelites of declaring a state of exception for purposes of warfare and state executions. Those deemed guilty of transgressions against the sovereign law, as well as those challenging its sovereignty, may be fought, persecuted, or simply eliminated.

Wars can never be surgically contained. There is always collateral damage, especially when entire cities are bombed without warning and innocent civilians are killed. But the state of exception may be applied to the innocent as well as the guilty, which again demonstrates that the ultimate power of true sovereignty is the power to kill anyone without remorse and without accountability—in other words, to transgress the very norms that allow ordered societies to exist in the state of generality..

Human Sacrifice

One of the most cherished illusions of modern societies is that human sacrifice is a thing of the past—in fact, the *ancient* past of Homeric legends, Aztec rituals, the Vedas, and the historical books of Hebrew Scripture. Did human sacrifice in fact disappear? Or did it just evolve and adapt? If the latter, then what form does it take in the modern world? To find out, we start by looking for instances where collectivities deliberately kill individuals or other collectivities. Having found a few, we ask, "What do all these lynchings, state executions, blanket bombings, Roman crucifixions, Capitol insurrections, and gang murders have in common besides violence?" The answer is that they are all in some way ritualized and structured to achieve their ends. In some instances, the participants' passions are aroused by incendiary rhetoric or strong sensory input—drums, chants, incense, torches, marching, dancing, etc.—while their inhibitions are often loosened by the ingestion of intoxicants and/or narcotics. At the same time, the collectivity is constrained by its own rules pertaining to the selection of the victim, the culture-specific symbolism of the sacrifice, the use of prophylactic measures to contain and channel the violence, and the elaboration of a mythology that will justify it.

These modes of structuring appear to suggest conscious intention, but in fact the persecutory crowd never has more than a superficial consciousness of them, as evidenced by their distorted memories of the event—e.g., the sorts of cognitive distortions that I listed at the beginning of this chapter, all of which assign guilt to the victim. When there is no one to point out these distortions, they become the dominant narrative known as myth. The role of the Sacred is to ensure that no one *does* point them out. It is the guardian of both the ritual and the myth.

ACTUAL MURDER

Human sacrifice is ritual murder—the deliberate killing of another human being as part of a process of social ordering. Whether it is spontaneous or planned matters less than the fact that it proceeds along lines that were laid down even before hominization occurred eight to ten million years ago. Rituals are instinctual in origin and have evolved to help people sort themselves out, build alliances and hierarchies, and manage themselves as viable groups for cooperative efforts. Like other instinctual processes, rituals are performed without any deep understanding of what ultimate purpose they serve, for understanding might raise awkward questions about them, rendering them less effective. They are performed with or without spontaneity. The important thing is that they are performed, because their beneficial effects are clearly felt even if their ultimate purpose is not understood.

Any group has an inside and an outside. The group attempts to maintain its equilibrium by expelling anything that threatens it. The expulsion may take many forms varying in severity, e.g., a group snub, a revocation of membership, a termination of employment, imprisonment, ghettoization, or extermination. We all keep our score sheets and know when we're pointing up or down.

So much competition for points may elicit strong negative affects like resentment, envy, hurt, jealousy, anger, and malice. Such emotions are rooted in our DNA but may be both shaped and triggered by the inherent mimesis of competition, where the desire to overcome the rival is revitalized with every defeat, every rebuff.

THE SACRIFICE

When levels of intra-group conflict reach a certain critical level, the group risks annihilating itself. This is the moment at which a sacrifice is likely to occur. All fears, guilt-feelings, and animosities converge on a victim whose expulsion then carries those negative affects away into the wilderness or the underworld.

Lynchings of Black Americans all over the US have abated but hardly disappeared. They have only evolved. "Lynching" is defined as killing, *but not necessarily* by hanging, as many people think. The scene of three Minneapolis police officers just standing by as a fourth one chokes a Black man to death is the scene of a lynching. Those Southern rednecks with their nooses *evolved* to become police officers with high-tech squad cars, guns, an appetite for violence against Black Americans, and just enough smarts to enter a profession that would present opportunities to satisfy that appetite legally. This is the path taken by two of the ultra-violent Droogs in Anthony Burgess's 1962 novel, *A Clockwork Orange*. See also my review of the 1950 *film noir*, *Where the Sidewalk Ends,* in Chapter 7.

A collective act of murder is ritual human sacrifice, regardless of whether it is performed within the law (as by firing squads) or outside it (as with lynchings). It is ritualistic because there are certain conditions to be met in order for it to be performed—e.g. , the selection of a suitable victim, getting everyone on board, and preventing ritual contamination, or blowback. Collective murderers intuitively understand these rules even when they do not recognize that they are performing a ritual of purification in which they will expel undesirable elements from their body politic. Even the Droogs had a body politic—even if it was rudimentary and fractious—and they had their rules— laid down, of course, by the alpha male.

Persecutory groups that are outside the law, like the Droogs, challenge the law's hegemony and may seek to overturn and replace it with their own if they can achieve critical mass. This happened in Germany in the 1930s when Nazi thugs came to power, and that scenario has been repeated, in one form or another, wherever states have been governed by strongman leaders.

In Britain's pre-Thatcherite society where the film's action takes place, the lawless are reabsorbed into society either by co-opting their violent tendencies (e.g. offering them jobs in law enforcement) or by rehabilitating them through various behavioral modification therapies such as the ones Alex undergoes.

It's important to remember that the Droogs *went looking* for victims. Finding a suitable victim was the first requirement for a successful ritual persecution. They started by beating up a poor derelict and worked their way up from there in Britain's class system. It wasn't just sport: they felt genuine malice for their victims, who represented either what they feared or what they desired. Expressing this malice together was a bonding experience for them.

But the Droogs were not very expert in conducting these rituals, because they failed to achieve unanimity and closure. These failures caused ritual pollution to occur: there was blowback in the form of guilt under the sovereign law.

The answer to our earlier question, "Is human sacrifice a thing of the past?" is an emphatic no. Human sacrifice has not disappeared and, on the contrary, we can read about it in every daily newspaper. It occurs in a long list of forms that include state executions, police killings, gang murders, lynchings, and the removal of legal protections for certain classes of people. Beneath its multiplicity of forms lies the anthropological identity that I have described.

VIRTUAL MURDER

A virtual analog to human sacrifice has always existed alongside the real thing. It is symbolic re-presentation of the ritual event through virtual performance. The analog is performed in songs, poems, novels, operas, plays, and movies.

The analog exists because it serves the same purpose as human sacrifice but without shedding anyone's blood. Its socio-psychological effects will vary according to a large number of factors, but, taken as a whole, they are adaptive in evolutionary terms, i.e., they persist for as long as they are useful to our species.

Sacred Ritual? ... Or Murder?

An explorer stumbles upon a jungle tribe in the process of immolating a man on a burning pyre. He approaches and shouts, "You can't burn this man! That's murder!" The natives reply through an interpreter: "But that's not a man. Can't you see it's a hyena? There's no murder here. This is a sacred ritual. Please remove your shoes."

We are forbidden to kill another human, but not another animal. Is the tribe's avoidance of the truth just a matter of metaphor, or is it a hallucination? Perhaps there is no difference between metaphor and hallucination in such rituals.

Witches in the DNC

Our job now is to soften up those three witches [Democratic officials] and make sure that we have

*good candidates to run against them, that they are
ready for the burning at the stake.*

—Ron Weiser, Chair of the Michigan GOP, in a speech of
03/25/21)

If everyone can be persuaded that these three Democratic officials are really witches, which is to say, demons, then sacred prohibitions against assassination do not apply. But in the modern day, it is very hard to pull off such a trick, though many may try. And in describing such an effort as a "trick," I do not mean to suggest that it is conscious. People who are highly excited do often hallucinate, and if they are excited together, they will tend to hallucinate together through a process of unconscious mimicry. Their susceptibility to each other or to a charismatic leader's influence facilitates the process.

Why might these distortions occur? Does faulty memory explain them? Memories are famously faulty when shaped by unconscious perceptual distortions such as group bias. Democrats and Republicans in the US still offer very different accounts of the 2020 election results and the insurgency of January 6, 2021. Children in the American South have been taught for over a century that the Civil War was fought over the issue of states' rights.

Our news media report conflicting claims about nearly every violent incident they cover. Rational thinking coupled with actual evidence can settle these claims in courts of law and elsewhere, but lacking those, conflicting claims are often settled by various forms of persuasion, such as appeals to scripture or tradition, charismatic leadership, propaganda, intimidation, and threats. By such means, any violent act can be framed so as to absolve its perpetrators. This is when misrecognition and disinformation take hold and come to be called "mythical" by those who know the truth.

Once again, we must not think of myth as limited to archaic societies. The so-called "Big Lie" of the 2020 Presidential election—i.e., that it was stolen from the incumbent—could not be a more explicit example of one.

Continuity of the Ancient and the Modern

Continuity is not identity. The modern world is plainly very different from ancient civilizations, yet many of the differences that we can identify share a common platform, or "deep structure," as Noam Chomsky might have described it. Zones of exclusion are universal. Every ordered society has its own way of creating them, as we have seen in the shift from polytheism to monotheism.

Analogies with species evolution are not misplaced. Although every adaptation is built on earlier ones, the earliest ones may be the most resistant to change simply because they are the most deeply imbedded and foundational.

What Neuroscience Tells Us

Our limbic system—also known as the emotional brain, the archaic brain, the instinctual brain, the unconscious brain, the hindbrain, and the reptilian brain—is everything that its descriptors suggest. It is responsible for our behavioral and emotional responses in matters pertaining, ultimately, to survival—feeding, procreation, fight vs. flight, caring for offspring, and social standing. (I include social standing because humans are social animals for whom expulsion is sometimes equivalent to death.) The limbic area lies just above the brain stem, whose evolutionary development began in fishes, predating hominization by hundreds of millions of years.

In humans, the cerebral cortex (aka, the rational brain, the cortical brain, the conscious brain, the forebrain, and grey and white matter) develops as the seat of consciousness and of any rational deliberation that we might be capable of. Behavioral endocrinologists have determined that actions that we consider to be under our conscious control are actually triggered by the interactions of hormones, the autonomic nervous system, and the limbic area of the brain microseconds before we are even conscious of any desire to perform them.

One implication of this finding is that we may largely unconscious of our true motivations and thus unable to accurately recognize our behaviors for what they are. Cognitive psychologists have identified over a hundred biases that continually shape our conscious perceptions of our own actions, driven as they are by pre-conscious impulses originating in the limbic system. The conscious brain can assess and process behavior, as well as strategize, but it cannot by itself generate behavior. Where bias is present, the conscious brain can either rationalize it or identify it as biased. The scientific method attempts to eliminate bias in the search for truth.

Another implication of the above findings is that self-deception—e.g., denial, guilt-shifting, and rationalization—is driven by fears of social death, which never bodes well for physical survival.

The prospect of death—whether physical or social—is terrifying. And because we have language, we are capable of constructing false realities, or fictions, about ourselves in order to maintain or improve our social standing, which is usually more important to us than we like to admit. In this process of denial and avoidance, the ethical and rational deliberations of the conscious mind are hijacked by unconscious fears of exclusion, expulsion, and death.

Our insights into these physiological processes have ramifications in every sphere of life. In the chapters that follow, I will revisit a few cultural artifacts that have caught my attention over the years—certain films, historical anecdotes, novels, etc.—in order to take a fresh look at them, this time through the lenses that mimetic theory and modern neuroscience provide. I am particularly interested in the murder mystery genre for its very readable plot lines and cathartic effects. I hope to show that those effects are achieved through ritual exclusion and that the drama is the actual ceremony representing that exclusion—a ceremony in which we, the audience, participate.

Chapter 4: Representations

Nomenclature

In the pages that follow, I will use a set of key terms in their broadest sense in order to encompass the multiplicity of their referents, for one of the purposes of this book is to show the unity of certain seemingly unrelated forms of human social behavior observed globally and across time. Such unities are often obscured by academic partitionings, superficial differences of content and form, competing perspectives, and our irrepressible cognitive biases.

COMMUNITY

I will use the word "community" to refer to any social group concerned with preserving its norms and protecting its boundaries. Like living organisms, communities maintain their equilibrium by incorporating what is benign and expelling what is malign (or perceived as such). "Community," therefore, includes a large number of types, such as clan, club, cohort, cult, country, street gang, primitive horde, religion, political party, or just "society"—meaning "societal norms." I will sometimes presumptively use the first-person plural pronouns "we" and "us," when I feel reasonably certain that my readers and I share the same basic moral and ethical norms.

AUDIENCE

I will refer to those who read, hear, or witness an unfolding story as its "audience," and I will often use the theatrical stage as a proxy for all media through which a story is communicated—even films and comic books.

NARRATIVE

Our uniquely human ability to represent ourselves *to* ourselves through the mirrors of narrative gives us the power to construct entire sagas about remembered or imagined human dramas.

Large or small, all dramatic narratives feature one or more foregrounded characters against a backgrounded community, even one that is invisible. Everything that happens in any story happens in a social matrix. What happens in drama is conflict.

CONFLICT

Conflict is, in fact, at the heart of every drama—and arguably of every narrative form including comedy—even when the adversaries work out their issues amicably, or when one of them is an impersonal force like fate or nature. Judging from box-office returns, many film audiences appear to favor stories about interpersonal conflicts that are resolved through some form of violence against one of the adversaries—e.g., imprisonment, suicide, murder, ostracism—even the derisive laughter of the stage community.

TEXT

I will define a "text" as anything that can be "read,"—not just written materials but also films, photos, paintings, stage plays, recitations, oral histories, and other media content, whether narrative or not. What interests me in narrative texts is the shape and structure of their stories—their "plots" rather than the media through which they're conveyed.

VIOLENCE

Context will help clarify whether I am talking about a "violence" that results in bloodshed or one that involves lesser forms of aggression all the way down to ridicule. In either case, a violent action is simply one that wounds.

Mnemosyne

Long before writing was invented, stories were most effectively and memorably told through live performances of dance, song, and role-playing. Because these performances were "live," no two would every be perfectly alike, and thus their stories were destined to evolve under the pressures of time and social change. The invention of writing offered a way to capture, preserve, and replicate versions of these evolving stories. Those versions—captured like snapshots at different moments—have become objects of interest to scholars attempting to trace the origins and filiations of different narrative structures and themes at different moments in time as well as across cultures.

Folk tales have always played an important role in community rituals, and in pre-literate cultures their preservation relied almost entirely on memorization. In ancient Greece, the goddess Mnemosyne, whose name is derived from the Greek word for "remembrance" and "memory," was mother of the nine muses, all of whom represented the recitative or performance arts— poetry (epic, love, and sacred), history, tragedy, comedy, music, dance, and astronomy, which, in ancient times, was heavily laden with stories of the gods and heroes. It's not hard to imagine why Mnemosyne would have presided over the muses, because mnemonic techniques such as rhythm and rhyme, chunking, images, and acronyms were essential to the faithful replication of all performances. However, she was no more capable of producing perfect copies than are the genes of living organisms.

Incarnations

What is true of folktales is also true of ancient myths and even "historical" accounts that originated in oral cultures and were later captured and preserved in writing. Measuring, tracking, and understanding a story's various incarnations through time and across cultures is impossible without "snapshots" of more than one version. Given enough data, we can identify the more durable deep structures in these narratives.

Scholars are also interested in the ways in which successive generations have understood these stories. Absent the possibility of interviewing audiences long since deceased, we can still tap into the prodigious resources of the human sciences in the 21st century and use existing data to form and test hypotheses. Philology, neuroscience, and cognitive psychology all contribute to this effort.

For example, we might want to know how much of a given story was considered by archaic audiences to be true. Could they distinguish between realistic elements and fantastical ones such as miracles, gods, and monsters? Did they know the difference between a lie and an illusion? Accumulated evidence suggests that these audiences had no concept of fictional narrative in ritual performance any more than they had a concept of secularism. All performance was ritualistic, and all narratives were about ancestors, local gods, heroes, and monsters. Their reality was not to be questioned lest the ritual spell be broken.

The notion that a story can be "just a story" may date back to Aesop's fables or earlier, but the audiences of ancient and pre- history, lacking basic scientific understanding of the world around them, were comparatively ill-equipped to separate truth from fiction, just as small children generally are. We now fully recognize the fictional nature of these fables because we know, for example, that animals like birds and fish don't use language to communicate with humans. But the fables may have evolved from earlier stories that featured totem animals interacting with humans. Those stories, in turn, may have resulted from perceptual distortions of events involving only humans—events in which some individual appeared to its tormenters as non-human—perhaps a minotaur, a cyclops, a dragon, or a hyena. This is convenient for the mythical memory machine, because ancient societal prohibitions against taking another's life (such as "Thou shalt not kill," the sixth commandment) do not apply to the killing of non-humans. The human realm does not protect the non-human realm from human-inflicted violence except when an animal is believed to be under the protection of a particular god. But such beliefs come and go, and the prohibition against killing humans remains. When such a prohibition is violated by some unauthorized individual or faction, it is called murder. When the prohibition is violated by the community, it is done ritualistically, and it is not called "murder." Rather, it is cloaked in euphemisms and myths provided by the first brain to obscure its truth.

The community's later mythical recollections of the event may feature a human metamorphosing into an animal or monster. This transformation is itself a ritual act, for it removes the designated victim from the community's protection and frees hisr persecutors to act with impunity.

Thus, the murder of a fellow human being can be transformed into something more benign by thinking of himr as non-human, sent by the gods to restore order and peace to a community that has been ravaged by plagues, internecine violence, droughts, or other disturbances—any of which may serve as the mythically distorted memory of a purely mimetic crisis.

At the time of its immolation, the sacrificed animal or half-animal is reviled for having caused all the troubles. Afterwards, it is honored for having carried those troubles away through its own death. Thus, a totem animal is born and may be regarded as godlike for the miraculous feat that s/he has performed.

This hypothesis does not exclude the possibility that the creatures populating animal fables are chosen for their resemblance to the humans they are meant to represent as well as for their power to evoke certain affects such as sympathy, fear, and disgust. Somewhere between myth and fable is a point where they meet.

Nor is this hypothesis only about archaic societies. If their patterns of social behavior were extinct, they would only be curiosities, not valuable resources for understanding what is happening in our world. Droughts plagues, and internecine violence still visit us in the forms of global warming, COVID-19, and political turmoil. Will our response be to turn on each other, as we've too often done? Will we demand more and more scapegoats in a bid to cap the spreading violence, and, when all the dust has settled, will we begin molding and shaping the memorial narrative about it in ways that will proclaim our own innocence and the guilt of the victim?

Makes and Remakes

We have all watched screen or stage adaptations of novels (e.g., *Les Miserables*, *The Age of Innocence*) as well as "remakes" of earlier films (*Breathless, Psycho*), so we know that stories can be carried on the chassis of more than a single medium or a single performance, interpretation, or production. And within a single medium like film, stories often reincarnate to suit the latest fashions and technologies.

Even mysteries are recycled in different versions, despite the likelihood that their audiences will know their outcomes in advance. Between 1955 and 2017, five films based on Agatha Christie's *Murder on the Orient Express* were released, and many moviegoers have seen more than one of them. The story has been periodically repurposed for different markets (e.g., the Japanese and German versions), or in response to changing fashions, cultural norms, and audience expectations.

A quick internet search turns up several hundred film productions that have been knock-offs, remakes, or parodies of earlier ones.

Narratives—much like language itself—are thus transportable through time and space; responsive to the changing needs and expectations of their audiences; generative—capable of producing subplots and spin-offs; and combinable into new genres such as the jazz musical or the magic realism of Jorge Luis Borges and Gabriel García Márquez.

Ritual Repetition and Morphing

The "makes and remakes" aspect of these stories suggests two conclusions. First, the audience does not *just* want to know what happened in the story any more than small children do ("Tell it again, Daddy!"). They like to go through it all again, even if they know the ending and can recite all the lines. Furthermore, they insist that it *must* be told exactly as before, with all the same dramatic effects. Catharsis followed by Daddy's kiss will ensure a good night's sleep. It is indeed the beginning of a lifelong pattern, for what's true of children is also true of adults: Through processes of identification (or "transference"), we enjoy the ritual recitation—the ritual performance—not as disinterested spectators but as impassioned participants.

This description applies to all narrative performance, including church liturgies, *Star Wars* movies, audio and printed books, and stage performances. The umbrella word for all these phenomena is "ritual." To equate narrative performance with ritual is only to say that they function in the same ways and serve the same core purposes. Both are symbolic representations that help us manage our emotions through transference. Both are re-enacted or re-presented again and again and share certain deep structures.

We know that there is a ritual quality to a narrative when we return to it again and again for its effects on our emotions, moods, and feelings. That narrative may take the form of anything between a Latin mass and *The Rocky Horror Picture Show*. The Agatha Christie mysteries lie somewhere between the extremes.

The second conclusion that I draw from "Makes and Remakes" (above) is that all narrative forms are as malleable as the cultural forces that shape them, but, like those forces, they must be structured in order to be intelligible and transmissible. Within that structure, an unlimited variety of representations can be made. Narrative, like language, is what psychologist Steven Pinker calls a "discreet combinatorial system." This means that, within a rule-based system, an infinite number of combinations is possible.

Successive live performances of a story are like the stream that can never be stepped into twice, for what they show us will never be visible again. Nevertheless, they allow us to track and analyze the changes that have occurred over time and to ponder their meaning.

Truth From Fiction

The early modern period in Europe (roughly, from Gutenberg through the sixteenth century) launched a powerful surge in humanity's understanding of itself and the world. Many such surges had occurred since ancient times, from China through India, Persia and the Levant to Europe. This one, however, was unprecedented in its ability to sustain and propagate itself through mass printing. Book publishers were sprouting up all over Europe and literacy rates were rapidly improving as more and more people were able to own their own books. Information and technology became exponentially more transmissible than ever before.

The pace of exploration, discovery, and innovation was breathtaking. Ships were circumnavigating the globe and exploring new lands. Painters were experimenting with perspective and achieving greater and greater realism. The competing cosmologies of semitic religions and ancient Greek astronomers were suddenly up against a formidable newcomer—Copernican heliocentrism, and Protestantism was challenging the Roman Catholic Church's hegemony over scripture and doctrine.

All these transformations involved discoveries of reality through careful observation of the material world. Everything, whether animal, mineral, or vegetable, became an object of observation. The habit of objectification extended to cultural phenomena, including politics, religion, and the arts.

No longer could anyone tell us that the man being sacrificed before our eyes was actually a hyena or that a crime of thought and belief was punishable by immolation. Individual judgment had been promoted as myth and dogma were demoted. The difference between truth and fiction might finally be recognized by individuals trusting their senses.

A fabricated story may pass for true—or at least, as the French say, *vraisemblable* (truth-like, plausible)—if its premises seem probable to any educated person born during or after the early modern era (16th century), when pre-modern stories about supernatural beings began to be regarded as fictional. This momentous transformation did not come painlessly, and it will never be complete, but it has had vast implications for our species.

It should be obvious that people who have reaped the benefits of a modern college education are on average better equipped than people with little or no education to distinguish truth from fiction in both scriptural and non-scriptural literature, the media, and political discourse. The educated tend to be more aware of cognitive traps and more practiced in certain mental disciplines necessary for getting to the truth. These are the rightful and laudable objectives of education everywhere. Moreover, when we compare the cognitive skills of 13th-century European elites with those of 21st-century elites worldwide, we find differences that are greater by several orders of magnitude. Both the educated and the uneducated cohorts of today are vastly more knowledgeable and capable of reasoning than their 13th-century counterparts.

What all this means for the art of the narrative is that, prior to the modern age, there was no reliable measure for distinguishing a true story from a fictional one. If one was instructed to believe something, it was true. If your tribal leaders said the man burning on the pyre was hyena, then you saw a hyena there and nothing more. Today, when we consider the cosmological claims made in the Bible, we know them to be untrue because we know the age of the Earth, we know that it is a sphere rather than flat, and we know that it is not at the center of the universe. How was a person to know these things in the 13th century? In fact, how was that person to know that Jews had not poisoned the wells, old women did not ride on broomsticks, and the world was not created by divine fiat? Anything was believable in an age that lacked modern methods of parsing truth claims, especially if it was also an age in which truth was not welcome.

Despite these differences in the way narratives are understood, we cannot fail to notice the structural resemblances between primitive narrative rituals and the narratives that we moderns like to play and replay. Each category features a performance and an audience, and each uses symbolic representations to plot sequences of meaningful actions. These plotted actions always exhibit certain contours of disturbance, and performance repetition is valued in both categories. Only time obscures the continuity of the primitive and the modern, and only time reveals their discontinuities. The way we "read" these narratives has changed much more than the narratives themselves.

Ancient Narrative, Modern Audience

Perhaps the most salient difference between primitive and modern narrative rituals concerns the community's "reading" of the narrative in question. By "community," I am referring to all those, both onstage and off, who witness and evaluate the onstage action performed by the protagonists. The onstage community is a participating audience, while the offstage audience may participate through identification with the onstage audience. The performance is an attempt to communicate a narrative to the audience via the performers' words and actions, and to somehow bridge the gap that always exists between stage and audience, speaker and listener. The gap exists simply because no two people ever experience anything in exactly the same way. Audiences are always diverse in their background knowledge, prior experience, interpretive skills, and cognitive biases.

Thus, the onstage audience, epitomized by the choruses in Greek tragedy, modern-day opera, and liturgical oratorios, persists in every drama as the larger community's commentary on the actions of the players. In an Agatha Christie mystery, the archetypal Greek chorus becomes the community of innocent stakeholders and suspects—and ultimately the judges and jurors who will deliver judgment against the accused. They represent the community whose peace and social order were disturbed and then restored following the expulsion of an individual or group held to be responsible, and we, the offstage audience, share the community's relief that justice has been done. The drama's deep structure—its cathartic passage from conflict to resolution—is what has kept us engaged.

The communications gap between characters onstage and spectators offstage offers many possibilities for variations in the narrative's surface structure. The characters know things that we don't know, they know things that other characters don't know, and we may know things that none of the characters knows. In addition to these differentials of knowledge, there are also differentials of interpretation, particularly as later audiences view productions targeted at earlier ones.

One thing that modern audiences want to know about stories predating the early modern era is whether they are true or partially-true accounts of real events. Was Oedipus a real person, and if so, did he really kill his father and marry his mother? And if he did, was he aware that they were his parents? We might conclude that the Oedipus story is plausible and possibly historical if its only themes were patricide and incest, but its plainly mythical elements, such as the protagonist's power to end the plague by solving the Sphinx's riddle, leave us to wonder if any of the events recounted in the story ever really happened. My habit of reading such stories starts with the postulate that myths are based on distorted memories of real conflicts that ended in some form of violence, from expulsion to murder. These distortions are neither random nor deliberate, but unconsciously purposeful, for they shield one of the parties in the conflict (a majority) from responsibility for having killed or expelled the other (a minority), and they allow peace to be restored.

Europe of the early modern period was not, of course, uniformly transformed by the progressive trends of the Renaissance. That period has left abundant documentation of the witch trials that were so common then. But while modern audiences can immediately recognize the persecutory nature of these trials, the authors of these documents could not, for they belonged to the community that was persecuting these women—a community consumed by fears of powerful malevolent spirits believed to inhabit human and animal bodies—a community unashamed of placing the accused woman on the burning pyre and unequipped to recognize its own delusions. The Jim Crow era bequeathed us numerous photos of lynchers so proud of themselves that they posed beside the corpse of the man they had hanged. (Just something to show the grandkids …) More recently, we have observed rioters filming themselves storming the US Capitol building while wearing clothing bearing their company's logo. These embraces of cruelty and abandonment of shame are so bizarre that they can only be described as hallucinatory.

Such a lack of shame over an actual or attempted act of lynching is a failure of both conscience and consciousness. Somewhere along the way, participants in these persecutions have lost the kind of moral framework that is essential if we are to understand the meanings of our actions. In the open societies of the modern world, such persecutions can never achieve their aim of cleansing and reordering the community. The ritual of sacrifice is always polluted by questions and doubts.

René Girard calls early modern accounts of scapegoating "texts of persecution." Our modern perspective allows us to easily spot their mythical elements and the persecutory nature of the scenes they describe, but early modern audiences were no more capable of doing so than were the lynchers of the Jim Crow era or the mob that stormed the US Capitol building looking for blood.

Our readings of these "texts of persecution" are prime examples of the gap that exists between modern audiences and pre-modern ones. These texts are snapshots not only of an actual event but of the audience's—and the scribe's—understanding of it at the time. While there is abundant evidence of the persecutions, there is no evidence that any of the charges against the victims were true and, in fact, those charges were often, by our standards of evidence, demonstrably fanciful.

Audience Participation and Catharsis

Like witch trials and other scapegoating rituals, the classic murder mystery is "successful" by the standards of the genre if it restores the social order of the fictional community while allowing the audience to participate vicariously in the accumulation and release of tension (the catharsis) occurring on the stage. The invisible "fourth wall" separating the fictional from the real world allows us to project ourselves into the drama as allies of the guiltless. We observe, approve, and participate in the fictional community's expulsion of the evil-doer, and, like that community, we feel relieved in the confidence that the expulsion has been effective and deserved.

Incontrovertibility in the Dénouement

The conventions of the mystery genre require that proof of the accused party's guilt be presented as incontrovertible. Lacking that incontrovertibility, guilt washes back toward the accusers along with the fear that they themselves may now stand accused. There may still be scores to settle, posing the risk of further disorder. The mystery genre in its classic form cannot allow any of this to happen. The dénouement (from the French *dénouer*, meaning to unknot) is expected to untie *all* the knots.

That is the privilege and the beauty of fictional writing. The murder mystery, whether in film or print, is an extreme abstraction of our own ongoing, imbricated, and tangled real-life dramas, all of which involve efforts to manage guilt and many of which never satisfy everyone involved.

Abstractions are reductive; they subtract anything regarded as non-essential to the core or essence of the object. Theoretically, it may be possible to reduce all classic murder mysteries to a simple plot line: a crime (murder) has been committed by someone in the community, everyone is under suspicion, and accusations fly back and forth until a third party—an inspector or detective—smokes out the murderer and reveals irrefutable proof of hisr crime. Punishment is administered off-stage by imprisonment, or on-stage by accidental death or suicide. To ensure a complete restoration of order, the mystery writer cannot allow any member of the community to be implicated in hisr death. The murderer himrself must appear to be the sole persecutor.

Some of the innocent suspects may have had the same motives, means, and opportunities as the guilty one, while others have been falsely accused. Though guilt has swirled around everyone's head, it has settled on that of a single individual or group, whose subsequent expulsion has carried it out and away from the community.

The classic murder mystery plot bears an uncanny resemblance to real-life scapegoating scenarios—but with one important difference. The scapegoat is believed by hisr persecutors to be guilty but is recognized by rational outsiders to be innocent, while the murder mystery convinces everyone—including ourselves, the "rational" audience—that the individual expelled from the community is in fact guilty. The integrity of the genre depends absolutely on this illusion. The murder mystery must not reveal that it is a ritual of virtual scapegoating. Otherwise, the ritual will fail. Thus, its standards of proof must be high enough to match those of audiences familiar with scientific methods of discovery. sports car Holmes could not have been imagined in a pre-scientific age.

The murder mystery is a genre for people who can recognize irrationality in the assignment of guilt and expect the investigator to pay scrupulous attention to facts in the interest of uncovering the truth. The evidence presented to the fictional community—and to the audience—must be convincing.

A murder mystery in which the star investigator ignores the facts or makes false inferences will not make the grade. Shoddy reasoning is reserved for a foil, usually in the person of a clueless police inspector. The methodological contrast between these two characters underscores the importance of truth to the integrity of the genre.

The murder mystery genre will never divide the chorus (the community) from the audience—at least not for long, for the former must ultimately serve as a projection of the latter. Both represent normalcy, even if the logic is something similar to "Since we see eye to eye, we must both be normal." An audience that does not successfully identify with the onstage community will not experience the intended cathartic effects. Much like tragedy, the classic mystery genre depends on catharsis—the purging of negative emotions like guilt, resentment, and anger.

"Purging" broadly means getting rid of whatever is impure or undesirable—not just from one's body and spirit, but from the body politic as well. The word "purge" occurs frequently in international news reports about autocracies holding onto power. In the mystery genre, the "purging" of the offstage audience's negative emotions closely tracks the purging of the onstage audience's (community's) own. Troublesome emotions are purged by expelling an onstage individual considered troublesome.

Like all narrative arts, the theatre and popular fiction have evolved out of archaic sacrificial rituals and the myths they represented and reaffirmed. This is only to say that every form and expression of narrative art is rooted in human sacrifice. It should *not* be interpreted to mean that human sacrifice is a thing of the past.

Sacrificial rituals can *only* be effective in cleansing the community of its own violence if *everyone's* aggressions are channeled toward a minority. There must be no stragglers and no one defending the accused, for otherwise, the gusher of violence will not have been securely capped.

The community that unanimously regards these myths as true accounts will be rewarded with closure—for as long as doubt doesn't creep in. From outside the community, the third-party "readers" of these re-enactments may recognize the arbitrary nature of their judgments, but the community's tendency will be to protect itself against such recognitions.

When we encounter a narrative that blames a minority for causing a plague or poisoning the wells, our modern instincts, shaped by the scientific revolution, tell us that it is a "text of persecution" because we can see that its causal links are broken. This is true whether the text is ancient or modern, written or performed,

When we encounter a text that convinces us—the children of the Enlightenment—that the minority is in fact guilty as accused, we have participated in a successful sacrificial ritual. Murder mysteries are, of course, closed systems contrived to lead audiences through an elaborate algorithm that can only lead to one outcome. Their manipulations are analogous to the scrupulous orchestrations of sacrificial rituals by priests since the dawn of humanity.

What can they offer us if not catharsis, purification, the satisfaction of seeing the guilty punished and the innocent vindicated?

Guilt Shifting in Murder Mysteries

A familiar climax for many murder mysteries has the ace detective gathering all the suspects and other stakeholders into one room, where he reconstructs the crime as he has concluded it occurred, explains the logic of his deductions, and finishes by revealing the identity of the murderer. Cornered and defenseless after having first denied hisr guilt, the assassin now confesses to killing hisr victim but—still in denial—is quick to add, "He made me do it!" or "He drove me to it," implying that the victim was in control and therefore responsible for hisr own death. Because hisr words express no contrition—only guilt-shifting—the assembled parties express no sympathy for himr—only relief— as s/he is led away by the police. Nor do we, the audience, have any qualms, for we have viewed the evidence and are satisfied that justice has been done. The guilty party did not even seek forgiveness, so we are not inclined toward mercy. We can now all breathe a sigh of relief and sleep soundly.

Agatha Christie Flips the Script

Agatha Christie's "Murder on the Orient Express" pushes the boundaries of her genre by depicting an onstage community (12 suspects) with which audiences will identify, then not identify, and finally identify once again. The success of the story will still depend on identification (aka, transference), but Christie will tease the audience in and out of it and, in so doing, test the limits of the audience's identifications.

A man named Ratchett is murdered in the sleeping compartment of his cabin on the Orient Express. Hercule Poirot—himself a passenger on the stalled, snowbound train—concludes from the trackless snow outside the carriages that the murderer is still on the train. There are 12 passengers besides himself and his friend M. Bouc, an official in the company that operates the *wagons-lits*.

So far, Christie appears to be writing another conventional genre classic in which Poirot will flush out the murderer, and everyone present will be relieved that the shadow of suspicion has passed over them. We expect the murderer will be handed over to the police and brought to justice, and s/he will carry away everyone's guilt.

But this is where Christie flips the script. Having gathered all twelve suspects into the dining room, Poirot does delivers an exquisite display of his observational and deductive powers in reconstructing the murder scene. But what he describes is a ritual murder carried out by all twelve of the suspects as revenge for Ratchett's earlier kidnapping and murder of a child to whom they were all attached. All twelve have serially plunged the dagger into Ratchett's body, expecting that their guilt for the deed will be equally shared and thus diluted—at least in their own consciences if not in the eyes of the law. But will we, the audience, agree that dilution makes the crime less horrible or that their victim's even more horrible crime justifies it?

Poirot's dramatic revelation amps up our revulsion toward Ratchett and draws our attention away from the twelve. We—the community, the audience—transfer *their* collective guilt into Ratchett's account, making him the persecutor and them the victims. So what is to be done with them? Are they to be turned over to the authorities? We now feel their pain and do not wish to see that happen. That leaves M. Poirot facing a moral dilemma *vis-à-vis* us and his conscience. Should he collude with the twelve and lie to the authorities or abide by the law and tell them the truth? Is it for him to show mercy and release them?

Let's not forget that Christie will have Poirot do anything she wishes him to do. And in this case, she has him "ratchet up" Ratchett's guilt from the outset. Before he is murdered, Poirot describes him as "an animal" and shows utter contempt for him in a face-to-face encounter. This sets us up for our later identification with Ratchett's assassins and Poirot's decision to advance a bogus theory about the incident when the authorities arrive. This is the point when some members of the audience may break the transference, but most do not.

Christie's script-flipping is a significant departure from the usual formula. Here, the murdered victim is himself a murderer, but his crime is the murder of a child—an act so horrific and unconscionable that his own death at the hands of the twelve avengers seems almost trivial. By colluding with them in a cover-up, Poirot and M. Bouc become part of the avenging-*cum*-persecutory crowd. We, too, may join the crowd by sympathizing with them rather than with their victim. This is a perfect scapegoating scenario, but we cannot see it because everyone in the crowd—Poirot, Bouc, the twelve, Christie, *and ourselves*—believes Ratchett to be richly deserving of his fate.

In a society governed by law, crowds that take justice into their own hands are called mobs, a desire for revenge does not justify a murder, and guilt is not diluted among multiple assassins. Christie knows this as she writes. But she has staked the success of her unusual, *genre*-bending narrative ritual on the audience's tendency to identify with the onstage community no matter what, and she does so by amping up the villainy of the victim and portraying the community of suspects—now murderers—as basically decent, god-fearing folks who deserve a break.

Poirot and M. Bouc model this interpretation for us and the onstage audience, and thus unanimity about the victim's guilt is fully achieved and the murderers are exonerated in the closed circle of audience, investigators, and, of course, the murderers themselves.

Christie has induced everyone—even Poirot himself, and us—to excuse the perpetrators for their violence instead of objectively recognizing what they represent. She has brought us right up on the stage to join the angry crowd, because unanimity about the cover-up will be of the utmost importance.

This is the way collective ritual violence occurs in primitive societies where the concepts of modern jurisprudence in a free society are as yet unknown. In a world where the principles of the Enlightenment have penetrated, every accused person is entitled to due process and is considered innocent until proven guilty. Even the most heinous crimes must be judged under the lens of the law.

Was Christie playing with her audience? Or was she testing, perhaps stretching, the scapegoating dynamic that drives the classic murder mystery? I am struck by the significance of M. Bouc's name. In French, *bouc* means goat. *Bouc émissaire* means "the goat that is sent out" (the scapegoat). Can this be coincidental? M. Bouc is not the scapegoat, but his name suggests that Christie was thinking along these lines and, like Rembrandt painting *The Night Watch*, may have planted a clue or two.

The Problem With Vengeance

Victims who survive persecutions—or their clans—often seek vengeance against the perpetrators. In so doing, they become perpetrators themselves, and thus the yin-yang of guilt and innocence spins on its axis, throwing off personal, ethnic, political, and religious feuds that may last for lifetimes or centuries. The feuding parties will imagine their differences to be both stark and obvious, but to an outside observer they are indistinguishable; both parties are victims and both are persecutors. Their violence has become cyclical, for every act of retaliation provokes another, and each party believes its violence will be "the last word" in the dispute. There are no clearer examples of this dynamic than the Arab-Israeli conflict, the long-standing Shia-Sunni feud, and the Catholic-Protestant schism in Northern Ireland.

In *Murder on the Orient Express*, the duodecet (the "twelve"), is a small community in a closed, stationary environment where the larger community cannot reach. What happens in that space stays in that space, at least until an equilibrium can be found. Only then can the train proceed on its way from the frozen wilderness back into the surrounding community.

This extreme isolation is necessary to protect the sacrificial ritual from pollution. Compressing the entire action into the confines of a passenger train certainly heightens the tension, but the hermetic sealing of the train also serves to hermetically seal the ritual against any reprisals that may be forthcoming–not from the victim or his allies, but from the civil authorities when the train reaches a city. There is an acute need for containment.

Christie's plot erases the clear boundaries that we expect the mystery writer to draw between victims and persecutors. Both Ratchett and the duodecet (representing the dead child) are victims, and both are persecutors (killers). We are watching a scene of reciprocal violence, tit for tat, that only ends when one of the antagonists (the duodecet) has the last word.

Is it justice, or is it vengeance? That depends on which of the two communities you ask—the train's passengers or the larger community to which they will shortly return. The problem of containment and closure is a challenge for Christie.

If no one is any longer innocent, then we are all—onstage and off—left with a bad conscience. The ritual has failed, for those who have exonerated themselves for murder can expect more disturbances to follow.

Christie could only avoid this outcome by declaring an exception to the conventional ethic of the mystery genre and playing up the difference between the antagonists. One is clearly portrayed as a monster—for only a monster would murder a child—and the other (the duodecet) is made to embody all the virtues of the European bourgeoisie or upper classes, as the case may be. It's obvious which of the antagonists Christie's readers would have identified with in 1934, the year the book was published.

My analysis is not meant to find fault with Christie but rather to point out the dilemma that this particular plot posed for her. Perhaps she was exploring an intuition that had occurred to her about one of the cardinal conventions of mystery writing—namely, that the difference between innocence and guilt, victims and victimizers, must be kept clear and strong. Perhaps this unusual plot was her foray into the sort of meta-genre that Dostoyevsky and many others had developed around the themes of crime and punishment.

In this case, the meta-genre would above all critique the genre and its conventions, but it might also better represent the messiness of real-life dramas in which culpability shifts around and reciprocal accusations are left to fester over lifetimes, staining everyone with feelings of guilt and resentment. And, whereas the mystery plot may have a very focused subplot or two, real life is usually throbbing with a variety of unfolding dramas. But, unlike the conventional mystery plot, real life dramas cannot promise catharsis of our negative emotions.

The audience's identifications with the characters in a cathartic drama compensate for the failures of catharsis in real life. Unable to manage our emotions productively, we carry around irritating residues of guilt, shame, and malice. So we return again and again to stories that conduct us through a purging process. This is what makes murder mysteries and several other genres so successful. They offer rituals of purification through violent expulsions that create or restore social order. This is no doubt a good thing, but these rituals come with a warning not to try them at home. The point of the ritual is to *channel* and *contain* violence so that it does not contaminate the space outside. The ritual is in sacred space, and the Sacred must above all maintain its monopoly over violence.

In archaic societies, these rituals were commemorative re-enactments of an actual, historical event that restored order to the community after a period of strife. "If it worked once," they said, "maybe it'll work again." Because the purge restored peace, it was replicated ritualistically at regular intervals based on the movements of heavenly bodies—sometimes with a human victim and sometimes with an animal proxy. For the sacrifice to be effective, there had to be a shedding of blood. No one bears ill-will toward grains and gourds.

Unanimous Distortions

Drawing a straight line between ancient sacrificial themes and an Agatha Christie mystery may still seem like a stretch until we consider two further similarities. One is the importance that both attach to community unanimity about the expulsion. As we shall see, the modern mystery drama is structured like real-life myths—both ancient and modern—whose purpose is to vindicate a majority for its spontaneous violence against an individual or other minority. The mystery drama has the advantage of being fictional, for it can be constructed so that the accused party is unanimously declared guilty and the climax affords everyone—on both sides of the fourth wall—a rush of righteous indignation, then the thrill of participating in a violent act mistaken for an administration of justice, followed by complete closure of the matter. Without unanimity, there is no rush and no thrill, and without closure there is no relief. In that case, a "ritual pollution" has occurred and negative emotions have not been successfully purged.

The ritual re-enactment is a form of narrative that we would now regard as mythical, not because it is based on an event that never occurred but because it reflects an interpretation that we can no longer share. When the myth tells the story of a boy who sang beautifully, but some people died of food poisoning after hearing him and so he had to be killed to restore their health, we quickly recognize the faulty reasoning that original audiences could not.

Despite such clearly mythical elements of stories labeled "myths," those stories are based on some actual event that has shaken one's own community. Through re-telling, that event is remembered and ritually re-enacted as a shared experience, not as a representation of a *type* of shared experience. But the community's memories of it are inevitably distorted because its members—like the mystery murderer—cannot see themselves as persecutors. If left unchallenged over time and across the generations, these distortions tend to wander farther and farther from the truth about the event. Primitive societies—particularly those pre-dating the invention of writing and those lacking systems of impartial law and justice—have left only residues for anthropologists to puzzle over. Those residues—usually in oral or written accounts—will never clearly implicate the persecutors, but they may acknowledge the victim's role in restoring peace to the community. This dynamic produces strange accounts of mythical heroes who appear, bring disorder or death in some form, die at the hands of the crowd, miraculously restoring social order through their victimage. Such victims are worthy of worship for the benefits their immolation has brought the community, while responsibility for the collective violence against them is mitigated, rationalized, minimized, displaced, or dispersed. Thus, all the pieces of the pattern fall into place as the victim is rehabilitated from trouble-maker to savior. The community cannot continue to revile himr, but neither can it afford to recognize hisr innocence. S/he is remembered both as a transgressor and a god.

To bring this back to home, the mythical distortions that have occurred in many Republican accounts of the January 6, 2021 siege of the US Capitol building—most notably, that the vice-president was a traitor and the insurrection was a false flag operation instigated by Antifa—are typical of the distortions that occur after all such events, whether in primitive societies or modern ones. These distortions develop into full-blown myths to the extent that the perpetrators are successful in controlling the narrative. Political power is the power to control the narrative about such events—whether to reveal the truth or to bury it. Authoritarian regimes are more invested in doing the latter.

Dilution, Erasure, Misapprehension

Participation in collective violence—the violence of mobs and gangs—dilutes each perpetrator's sense of individual responsibility and provides cover and support for more extreme behavior. All the better if the authorities turn a blind eye to it—in effect erasing it-–as happened in Germany under Nazi rule and in communities of the American south for a hundred years after the Civil War. We observe this pattern today in the Russian Federation, in most of the predominantly Muslim societies, and in certain "Christian" areas of Africa, where sexual minorities are actively persecuted and deprived of legal protection against assault and murder.

The inciters and perpetrators of violence rarely if ever admit wrongdoing immediately after their deed—not because they are consciously lying but rather because they believe they have done nothing wrong and that their victims are guilty and deserve the punishments they've received. These perceptual distortions are not unlike hallucinations. The victim is transfigured into something inhuman, monstrous, and evil, as we saw when Poirot described Ratchett as "an animal." In archaic communities, a second transfiguration typically occurs later when the perpetrators come to view their departed victim as a god in disguise.

The hallucinatory misapprehensions of the perpetrators are in fact what makes their violence possible. They do not understand what they have done.

Recognition and Conversion

These irrational and non-conscious elements are always present in scapegoating and do not dissipate until the spell is broken and the perpetrators recognize that they are persecutors. Not long after Jesus's death, Paul the Apostle, whose Hebrew name was Saul of Tarsus, persecuted disciples of Jesus until he experienced a vision while on his way to Damascus to conduct a purge. According to his own account, he was blinded by a bright light and heard the voice of Jesus saying to him,

"Saul, Saul, why persecutest thou me?" His recognition of himself as a persecutor rather than an avenger is neatly symbolized by the restoration of his sight.

The Hebrew scriptures frequently vindicate the victims of slanders and scapegoating, notably in the stories of Cain and Abel, Joseph and his brothers, Joseph and Potiphar's wife, and Job. In the Passion of Christ as recounted in the Gospels, the intuitions expressed in those earlier prophetic and narrative traditions come into focus as never before. The sacrifice fails because a small group of dissenters who cannot be persuaded of the victim's guilt build a movement that will not only declare his innocence but reveal the mechanisms of his persecution as they have understood them.

The Gospel writers did not agree in every particular about what had happened to their master. They were writing decades after the events they describe, and there is no evidence they were eyewitnesses. Their accounts were then subjected over an entire millennium to all the forces that can erode a text that is only propagated through hand-copying and translation. Nevertheless, the main framework of the Passion narrative is still visible.

Fundamentally, the aggregated Passion stories depict a community starkly divided in response to a crisis. That crisis is Judea's occupation by Roman armies, which is perceived as an existential threat to the nation.

The Jewish authorities (the Sanhedrin) have recognized the futility of resistance and accepted the necessity of Roman rule. Their challenge is to maintain the country's internal stability for as long as the Romans occupy its soil. The consequences of not doing so could be annihilation.

These conditions are ripe for factionalism among the Jews. The Roman occupation is brutal, and yet the religious authorities are accommodating it. In outlying areas, sects are forming around charismatic leaders like John the Baptist and Jesus. They are denouncing the formalism and rigidity of the priests and offering a salvation that is not of this world to a people hungering for hope. Crowds are forming around these wandering preachers, and the authorities are nervous.

The priestly class regards Jesus as an outlaw who threatens both national security and the sacred order as they know it. They plot Jesus's death, and Caiaphus, the chief priest of the Sanhedrin, provides the rationale. Here is John's description:

> *Therefore many of the Jews who had come to visit Mary, and had seen what Jesus did, put their faith in him. But some of them went to the Pharisees and told them what Jesus had done.*
>
> *Then the chief priest and the Pharisees called a meeting of the Sanhedrin. "What are we accomplishing?" they asked. "Here is this man performing many miraculous signs. If we let him go on like this, everyone will believe in him, and then the Romans will come and take away both our place and our nation."*
>
> *Then one of them, named Caiaphas, who was high priest that year, spoke up, "You know nothing at all! You do not realize that it is better for you that one man die for the people than that the whole nation perish."*
>
> *He did not say this on his own, but as high priest that year he prophesied that Jesus would die for the Jewish nation, and not only for that nation but also for the scattered children of God. So from that day on they plotted to take his life.*
>
> (John 11:45-53 NIV)

It is Better That One Man Die

Caiaphus's words reveal a timeless truth about scapegoating. It is that nothing brings quarreling neighbors together like a common enemy—someone who can be blamed for everything and whose elimination will make everything better. And what can be more productive of unity than a common purpose?

In archaic societies, the only common purpose guaranteed to unify the entire community is sacrifice—spontaneous or ritualized murder. But it only works if everyone mimetically believes it is something else and find a rationalization for it. It doesn't matter who the common enemy is, but if there isn't one, then one will be found. This is why Girard suggests that the choice of a sacrificial victim is basically arbitrary: It doesn't matter *whom* one crucifies; what matters is the crucifixion itself, for it alone will "save the nation."

Caiaphus knows this, of course. First, he spells it out, then he cynically prophesies that Jesus will die for the Jewish nation, all of which is tantamount to announcing that there will soon be a sacrifice and the only patriotic thing to do is join the frenzied mob. This would explain why the crowds that first welcome Jesus into Jerusalem soon turn on him. The high priest's prophesy—akin to a press release or a leak in today's world—names the victim and supplies the myth, and the crowds takes it from there.

The disciples experience a kind of rolling recognition of what is unfolding before their eyes. They are so imbued with Jesus's teachings that they can finally see these events almost as plainly as he himself sees them. Thus it has been claimed that the Passion story is paradigm-shifting, revealing the mechanisms of scapegoating re-presenting the sacrificial crisis as seen from the perspective of a victim who fully understands what he is walking into and yet accepts it as a sacred mission.

Jesus's disciples could not have saved him through any efforts of their own—the Roman soldiers would have been only so happy to erect a few more crosses—and so they had abandoned him, just as he had predicted they would. Only Judas actually conspired with the authorities against Jesus, while the others capitulated to the mimetic power of the mob by denying any knowledge of their master.

This was a powerful teaching moment for the disciples. Jesus had prepared them well for their role as future propagators of his message, and the events of that week seared it into their consciousness. He did this by loving them and binding them to him at every opportunity with promises of eternal life in return for belief in him and his message. This was truly a charismatic cult, regardless of its merits. When its leader died, the survivors carried on his work.

The history of Christianity shows how fragile and fleeting the disciples' *a posteriori* recognition was. Christians and their institutions, while originally exalting the victim, too often became persecutors themselves until their hegemony was broken by secularism. Recognition of the kind that Paul experienced on the road to Damascus seemed at times to have been forever extinguished. And yet, Judeo-Christian scriptures carried forward the theme of the innocent victim, leaving it to do its glacially slow work of raising our consciousness about scapegoating. That awareness has appeared in some of the Western world's greatest works of literature, from Othello's recognition of Desdemona's innocence, to Raskolnikov's repentance in Dostoyevsky's *Crime and Punishment*, and Briony's recognition of her guilt in Ian MacEwan's novel, *Atonement*. That awareness has also spun off legal and judicial systems dedicated to protecting the innocent from persecution.

Conscience and Consciousness

Our words "conscience" and "conscious" are very close in meaning. Both are derived from the Latin *con* (with) and *scientia* or *scios* (knowledge). Scapegoating is a failure of both conscience and consciousness because it rests on a lie that takes itself for the truth. As I explained in Chapter 1, neuroscience has ascertained that the second and third brains (the emotive and the mimetic brains) activate impulses before the first brain (the rational brain) has any knowledge of them. The rational brain can then block them or let them through, all the while crafting justifications to handle the social consequences of either response. Those justifications are themselves shaped by the mimetic and emotive brains, producing elaborate skeins of truth and falsehood, guilt and innocence.

Nothing gnaws at the soul like guilt. Since no one likes carrying it around, our tendency is to shake it off by any means possible and at every opportunity. Human culture has always provided abundant means for doing so, and among them are denial (to oneself and others), confession (provided that it is followed by repentance and forgiveness), and scapegoating, which amounts to ritual blame-shifting. In certain situations, of course, a confession results in an accumulation of guilt and a feeding frenzy of scapegoating.

Denial and scapegoating cannot effectively rid us of guilt unless they are unconscious. We cannot allow ourselves to understand what we are doing because we need to believe that we are innocent. Our belief in others' guilt is built on the same shaky foundation. A sacrificial ritual serves to transfer everyone's guilt onto a single individual or minority, but it can only succeed if the community absolutely believes it has done the right thing. The objective is to feel cleansed and righteous after the sacrifice, not to create a new source of guilt.

Lynching

"Folks! Folks! Quiet, please. Listen up! The county sheriff's comin' down here pretty soon. Well, you and I all know he's a real nosy guy, and he'll be askin' all kinds of questions about what happened out there at the edge of town last night. So listen up! We gotta make sure he hears only one story. I repeat, one story! If we start arguin' and disagreein' about what happened, we're back in the bog. So listen to me carefully! Here's what really happened as I see it, and if you thought you saw something else, you were just dreamin'.

It seemed like all our troubles started when that stranger hit town. He didn't seem to have any friends and he just kept to himself. I figure he must have poisoned the stump water because we all started actin' mighty peculiar after he got here. Know what I mean? Remember how irritable and quarrelsome we were? It's like everybody was eatin' bottle caps and broken glass for breakfast. Why, old Tom and Charlie just about killed each other over somethin' they don't even remember. Then Charlie's wife showed up battered and dead in a ditch and somebody said it was that stranger guy that mighta done it. We looked for him everywhere, but he'd just gone and disappeared.

Then his body was found hangin' from a tree at the edge of town. He was beaten up pretty bad. Gotta wonder who coulda done a terrible thing like that... But we all feel a lot safer now, don't we?"

Catharsis as a Function of Representation

Catharsis is a measurable mimetic and physiological response to a representation of scapegoating, which I have defined as a transfer of community guilt to a victim through an act of persecution that may result in the victim's death or exclusion. This transfer may occur within the juridical order or outside it—in the courtroom, the barroom, or the streets of the fictional narrative.

Catharsis is the function and purpose of the representation and can only be achieved under certain conditions that correspond very closely to the prohibitions and requirements of archaic sacrificial rites. Chief among these requirements are unanimity and closure.

UNANIMITY

The community that has been disturbed undergoes a spontaneous purge and re-ordering around the unanimous expulsion of whomever can *successfully* be blamed for the disturbance. This is not a conscious process. The path toward unanimity begins when one of two antagonists finds an ally in a third, for then a fourth and a fifth are likely to join their coalition—not for any rational or conscious reason but because of the dominance of their position in relation to the accused. In mimesis as in planetary physics, the greater mass of larger bodies allows them to exert a greater force of attraction than those with smaller mass. Like many other species, we humans are instinctually wary of separating from the "larger body" that envelops and protects us. Add to that our capacity for mimetic interdividuality and you get human culture with all its glories and faults. We get rampaging mobs . . . but we also get symphony orchestras.

This dynamic helps explain a host of awkward social situations in which one is expected to behave in ways contrary to one's own values or judgments. As one example, contagious laughter is triggered, not by something funny, but by the laughter of others. Everyone else is laughing, so it must be funny. If you're not laughing, you don't "get it," or you must be having a bad day. In mimetic terms, the discomfort that comes with being the only one in the group not laughing is no different from that of an outsider, or third party, who is present during a lynching and cannot succumb to the hallucinations driving it. Other common and familiar examples include social pressures bearing on individual participation in group activities such as the sharing of food, religious observances, political expression, committee meetings, and, of course, wartime combat. All such scenarios depend on mimetic unanimity and suppression of individuality.

None of this amounts to saying that mimetic unanimity is inherently problematic. Unanimity about climate change and COVID-19 is highly desirable, whether it's mimetic or not.

CLOSURE

Unanimity about the guilt of the victim brings closure to the social drama. There will be no reprisals, no lingering embers of discord, no doubts, and no further questions. We'll all leave the scene (*la scena,* the stage) feeling better than before we entered it.

Dramas that can successfully carry most audiences along on this arc (through transference, or identification) create the conditions necessary for catharsis to occur. For many audiences, this is easily accomplished by setting up clear "good-guy, "bad-guy" polarities, as in the James Bond movies and *Raiders of the Lost Ark*. All the better if the villains are monsters threatening civilization itself, as in *King Kong* and *Godzilla*. Such films are un-self-consciously and efficiently ritualistic because they are scripted for the sole purpose of facilitating catharsis by the most direct means possible for audiences with little patience for moral ambiguities.

Guilt-Shifting

It's important to remember that all such stories are symbolic representations of guilt-shifting and that we watch them because we want to vicariously experience the extreme polarization and then expulsion that they represent to us—as long as we ourselves are not the ones expelled. I am, in effect, saying that we, the audience, are the persecutory crowd because of our identifications with a stage full of characters who become polarized against a single individual or minority whose guilt they—and thus we—will regard as incontrovertible. And if the crowd requires no further investigation, then neither do we. We'll take their word for it because we trust them. That is what we expect to do when we participate in this ritual. We want to form and sort out our identifications with characters both good and bad; we want to join their pursuit of the one person who, as everyone can agree, is unquestionably guilty, and who, once identified, must be purged from the community.

It's guilt-shifting that we want to witness—the transfer of all guilt onto one person or more. That person carries the collective guilt out of the community and out of our living-rooms and theaters through hisr actual or social death. The community is relieved, and so are we.

And how else would it be? A proper murder mystery cannot even exist without the structuring of guilt that I've described. This genre exists because its spectators want to experience the good vibes that crowd-immersion produces when it leads to unanimity about someone's guilt and subsequent punishment.

The pattern I've described is common not just to the murder-mystery genre but also to others, like horror, sci-fi, fantasy, adventure, and war, in all of which the designation and elimination of some feared Other predictably drives the action. The whole point of all these genres is absolutely the same, i.e., to make us feel safe and morally cleansed after the performance. The most time-honored, indeed primal, method of providing this service for the audience is to stir up their emotions and then manipulate the release of those emotions. through participation in a ritual sacrifice of a chosen victim. The transferences that occur between stage and audience are dialed up or down, encased in irony, complicated by love, and layered within subplots. But it's a rare story that doesn't involve—or dare I say, depend on?—a transference of guilt, even if it's guilt-lite, followed by repentance and atonement.

Conversion Stories

I have a particular fondness for film stories in which guilt is on the prowl for a victim but never settles on anyone because everyone involved eventually recognizes hisr own judgments and retributive impulses for what they are and determines not to inflict them on others. These are what many literary critics call "conversion" stories, i.e. stories of personal transformation, initiation, coming-of-age—and they are, I think, a pleasant counterweight to stories that follow the sacrificial route all the way to violent catharsis. And yet the transformation always involves pain—the pain of rebirth, of shedding the old self and embracing the new.

René Girard made a useful distinction between romances and novels in one of his first books, *Mensonge romantique et vérité romanesque*, translated literally as "Romantic lie and novelistic truth." (The English translation was given the title, *Deceit, Desire, and the Novel.)* The Romantic lie is obedient to the demands of cathartic ritualistic violence for unanimity and closure. The novel, as Girard defines it, invites us to detach ourselves from the ritual and view it from the outside. In this way, the novel hastens the dissolution of the Sacred, which depends for its efficacy on misrecognition of its foundations in violence.

Chapter 5: Guilt and Innocence in Fritz Lang's Films Noirs

In Chapter 2 (Mimesis), I used the plots of five Hollywood movies to illustrate various forms of mimesis. In the previous chapter, I asserted that all dramas are symbolic representations of guilt-shifting through a process that begins with identifications (or transference) and ends in catharsis. I would now like to examine the plots of eight *films noirs*—all either directed, produced, or scripted by Fritz Lang, and all featuring a murder.

First in Germany, then in Hollywood, Fritz Lang produced dozens of social dramas exploring the moral ambiguities inherent in the relation between outsiders and the law. Lang was partly Jewish and thus acutely sensitive to political currents in Germany before and after he fled from there in 1933. The Nazi Party had recently banned Lang's most recent film, *The Testament of Dr. Mabuse*. Nevertheless, they were impressed with his abilities and saw him as a potential recruit for their propaganda efforts. Hitler's Minister of Propaganda, Joseph Goebbels, invited Lang to his office and offered to make him the head of UFA, the German film studio. Lang reminded him that, under the Nuremberg Laws, his official classification was "partly Jewish." Goebbels reportedly answered, "*We* will decide who is 'partly Jewish.'" Lang fled the country that every evening.

Lang was, first of all, a highly literate and perceptive man with a keen interest in the psychology of crowds and the techniques of propaganda used to manipulate them. His success in filmmaking rested largely on his keen observations of human nature and his need to understand and truthfully report what he observed, for all of Europe seemed poised for years of cataclysmic violence—in mimetic terms, a sacrificial crisis that was to end in scapegoating on an unprecedented, genocidal scale.

The first of his films that I will discuss appeared in 1931, and the last one in 1954. I haven't included any of his four anti-Nazi films—*Manhunt, Ministry of Fear, Hangmen Also Die!,* and *Cloak and Dagger*—because they were tailored to serve the Allied war effort.

All nine of the films that I have selected explore issues of guilt, innocence, blame, vindication, the law, and justice. Though it's probably safe to say the same about all *films noirs*, Lang's lifelong preoccupation with these themes infused his entire *oeuvre* and gave it coherence and depth.

M (1931)

Lang's 1931 German film *M*, starring Peter Lorre as Hans Beckert, is about scapegoating and mob violence in a way that few other films have ever been. Lang does not want us to feel easy about murder, even when it is in retaliation for a previous murder or other crime. It doesn't matter whether the murdered victim is innocent or guilty.

A serial child murderer (Beckert) is on the loose, and the police are roughing up the criminal underworld where they expect to find him. But Beckert is an outsider even to the outsiders. Their various warring constituencies—extortionists, drug dealers, prostitutes, etc.—decide to put aside their differences and cooperate in identifying, capturing, and executing him. The police, on the other hand, are determined to bring him to justice. Beckert successfully eludes his pursuers until he slips up, allowing the mob to corner him in the attic of a commercial building. They haul him into a subterranean enclosure where he is brought before a crowd of underworld characters to face their denunciations. There are no intermediary or intercessory characters of the sort you would find gathered around defendants in a legal trial. Beckert stands utterly alone facing the crowd.

He pleads with his persecutors to understand that he has no control over his impulses and needs medical help. His speech reminds us that he is protected by law from spontaneous retributive violence and that there is a humane alternative to what the mob is intending to do. They, however, are unmoved by his words and are about to tear him limb from limb. At the last moment, they stop in their tracks as a man emerges from the shadows behind Beckert and places a reassuring hand on his shoulder. Lang's cinematography keeps the focus on Beckert's terrified expression and allows us only to see the newcomer's hand and hear his voice. The hand symbolizes benign political authority in an ordered society. The man's words plainly state the moral of the story, which is about the truth of justice and the lie of mob violence. The persecutory crowd comes to its senses in a scene that is almost sacramental.

Lang's ending for *M* is not unlike William Golding's ending for *Lord of the Flies* (published in 1954 and adapted for film in 1963), in which a mob of English schoolboys, stranded on a desert island after their plane crashes into the sea, have reverted to savagery and are pursuing one of their fellows with the intent to kill him.

At the critical moment, a surprising intervention occurs. Their fleeing victim falls in the beach sand and looks up to see the spotless white shoes and trouser legs of a British naval officer. The very sight of this man, symbolizing as he does the rule of law in an ordered society—stops the pursuers in their tracks and brings them to their senses. The religious overtones in this final scene are inescapable, for we are made to witness one of the most primitive expressions of the sacred— spontaneous mob violence against an innocent scapegoat. Comparisons with *M* are not misplaced, for its final scene reminds us that Beckert is innocent until proven guilty in a court of law. In both these films, the sacrifice is aborted by a *deus ex machina* representing— as gods always do—the sovereign social order. The schoolboys' attempt to create their own sovereign social order through acts of violence is interrupted by a man— a military officer, no less—representing a society that sometimes asserts its own right to arbitrary violence.

In both films, a marginal group attempts to further marginalize and expel another individual who will carry away their collective guilt. Lang's choice of a criminal underclass to persecute another criminal suggests that their own burden of guilt is a major factor in their rage against him. The mob of schoolboys in Golding's tale are already guilty of murdering one of their schoolmates when they set upon his friend to kill him as well. Here we see a concern with unanimity around a sacrifice that has already taken place. Anyone who remains apart from their little mob will pollute the sacrifice by interrupting their transfer of guilt. Hisr very presence will be a reproach to them.

In both stories, the only reason the intended sacrifice fails is that the mob does not enjoy the state's monopoly on violence and thus has no secure enclosure for its own violence. Where that enclosure does exist, as in the sovereign state, it is called the Sacred, even when that sovereign authority is putatively secular or even godless. The resemblances between Soviet communism and the Orthodox Christianity that it expelled have been noted by many observers. Every essential component of that religion was preserved in the Soviet order that followed it—deified leaders (Stalin, Lenin), holy books (the Communist Manifesto), pilgrimages (e.g., to Lenin's tomb), myth (propagated through a state monopoly of media), suppression of individuality, persecution of heretics (dissenters), and, above all, unquestioning faith (the imperative of groupthink in a totalitarian society).

Fury (1936)

Like Agatha Christie's *Murder on the Orient Express*, Fritz Lang's 1936 film *Fury* inculpates the persecutory crowd. (In *Murder* ..., the "crowd" was the twelve suspected passengers on the train.) But while Christie's script does so only momentarily before transferring the crowd's collective guilt to their victim (because he is incalculably worse than they), Lang's script carries the crowd's guilt through to the end, and their victim is portrayed as innocent from the start. This film also makes an interesting contrast with Lang's earlier film, *M*, where both the crowd and the victim are guilty to the end.

Joe and Katherine (Spencer Tracy and Sylvia Sidney) are engaged to be married. On his way to meet her in a distant town, he is stopped by a deputy sheriff and questioned. The police in that county are looking for suspects in a recent child kidnapping case. Joe is taken in and questioned further. On the basis of some very circumstantial evidence (e.g., his habit of carrying peanuts in his coat pocket), he is held in the county jail.

Rumors start to fly in the community, and soon everyone agrees, on the basis of hearsay alone, that Joe must be the kidnapper. A torch-bearing lynch mob forms in front of the jail. Despite the sheriff's resistance, the mob storms the building. Unable to break into the cell block, they retreat to the outside and set the building afire. Katherine arrives just at the moment when someone has thrown dynamite into the building. She sees Joe clutching the bars of his cell window, screaming for help as the flames engulf him, and she faints.

Several days later, Joe shows up at his brothers' apartment. Somehow he has escaped the flames and fled the scene. He is bitter and wants revenge on his persecutors. He plans to remain in hiding until after the mob's participants are all tried and executed for murder. Katherine is not to know.

The brothers pay a visit to Katherine, who is traumatized and speechless. They do not reveal that Joe is still alive, but Katherine notices that one of them is wearing the same coat that Joe was wearing when he set out on his trip. She says nothing but becomes alert to further clues that Joe might be alive.

In the courtroom, the defendants are so numerous that they have crowded out the spectators. In symbolic terms, they are the community itself, or a subset thereof–a community tried for murder by a larger and more authoritative community asserting its sovereignty. All these defendants deny that they were present at the scene of the riot, and none will testify against any of the others. Their unanimity holds until some newsreel footage surfaces, showing their faces very clearly.

Katherine discovers additional clues that Joe is alive, and she finds him in his brothers' apartment. He is no longer the happy-go-lucky fellow he used to be. His sole obsession is revenge, but she cannot be persuaded to to share it with him. Katherine leaves disappointed but still hopeful.

The perpetrators are found guilty and, just as their sentence is about to be read to them by the judge, Joe enters the courtroom and approaches the bench. There, he delivers a stirring speech about how he almost lost faith in his fellow man. The defendants will not serve life sentences or face execution. Joe and Katherine are reunited.

Lang's tale is much less forgiving of the persecutory crowd than Christie's, but both appear to ponder the question of how a crime of murder is to be judged when it is committed collectively by a crowd. It matters little that Christie's crowd (the twelve of them) have murdered the kidnapper and murderer *of a child*, or that Lang's crowd has attempted to murder a man *thought* guilty of kidnapping a child. Both stories attempt to avoid a complete reversal of the usual dynamics of guilt, because the punishment of a murderous crowd opens up a perilous political dimension that the stories tend to avoid. Prosecution by the state of an entire crowd of people greatly multiplies the chances that their violence will not be capped but instead spark reprisals.

These two stories have demonstrated the importance of closure at the conclusion of the sacrificial ritual, as well as the immense difficulty of reversing the usual polarity of community innocence and victimary guilt. *Murder on the Orient Express* "succeeds" only by relying on Hercule Poirot's impeccable *gravitas* to legitimize his circumvention of the law. And yet, we are left with an uneasy feeling that his cover-up is not quite kosher.

Until its final scene, *Fury* appears to be heading in the same direction but by a different route. An act of horrific violence has been perpetrated by a mob taking justice into its own hands, and now Joe, too, seems intent on taking justice into his own hands by letting the mob take a rap for murder when no murder has actually occurred. Only Katherine's intercession stops his descent toward an act of vengeance that would forever haunt him with guilt.

You Only Live Once (1937)

Lang's 1937 film, *You Only Live Once*, followed close on the heels of *Fury* (1936), and it, too, features Sylvia Sydney, now paired with Henry Fonda. Both films depict persecutions as seen from the perspective of the victims, but their outcomes are very different.

Ex-con Eddie Taylor wants to stay clean and out of trouble. Before serving his three-year term, he and Joan had married, and now they are trying to buy a home and start a family together. He has found a job driving a truck, but his boss—a sadistic individual—has apparently hired him just for the pleasure of firing him. Stigmatized by the community as an ex-con, Eddie can't find another job and is unable to make the mortgage payments. Now desperate, he appears to be contemplating a heist.

Then a heist does occur and four security guards are killed. Eddie knows the police will soon arrest him, but he swears to Joan that he didn't do it. He is captured and sent back to prison by the governor's orders, this time to face execution. Embittered and refusing to accept his impending death, he attempts to break out and takes one of the prison officials hostage. He is in a tense standoff with the armed guards when the warden receives a telegram from the governor. The real robber has been found, and Eddie is thereby pardoned.

However, Eddie believes it's all a trick and refuses to release his hostage. The prison chaplain, whom Eddie has previously trusted, tries to show him the ticker tape, but Eddie doesn't believe him either. Eddie escapes, but only after unintentionally shooting and killing the chaplain in a tussle.

Eddie and Joan, who is about to give birth to their child, attempt to flee to Canada. It is a perilous journey, with the police on their trail and the locals on the lookout for them. Their son is born under a tree just off the road, and then they continue their flight. Joan's sister lives up ahead, so they leave the infant with her.

The police catch up with the couple just as they are approaching the Canadian border. Joan is wounded when an officer sprays their car with machine-gun fire from behind. The car runs off the road, and Eddie carries Joan in his arms toward the border. Officers carrying rifles pursue them, and, just as Joan breathes her last breath, one of them shoots Eddie in the back—from afar, as though the man in his gunsights were wild game.

JOE VS. EDDIE

In *Fury*, Joe is just an ordinary Joe, a happy-go-lucky guy who is in love with his fiancée and seems destined for happiness and success. Eddie is another matter, for he is already marked as an ex-con and can expect to swim upstream for the rest of his life. And then there's Joan, who is as innocent and as faithful to him as Katherine is to Joe.

Joe's conscience is nearly hijacked by his outrage, but it prevails as proof of his strength of character. Though he initially seeks vengeance against his persecutors, he renounces it just as it comes within his grasp. Closure is achieved not through a sacrificial act (his persecutors' convictions for murder) but by his refusal to have any part in one.

Eddie, though good-hearted, is not a saint. He has renounced violence while in prison, but, now free, he resorts to it again when his life is at stake. Faced with imminent electrocution, his autonomic fight-or-flight responses merge into a desperate fight to flee at any cost. The chaplain is the price for his brief freedom.

Joe is a scapegoat to whom circumstances have awarded an opportunity to take revenge, and he declines the privilege. Eddie never reaches any such point, for he is on the run until he's killed. He is fleeing just as Joe might have done if he had not been imprisoned in the burning courthouse. Would Joe have taken a gun in hand and used it?

Perhaps there is no real difference between Joe and Eddie. It's only their circumstances that differ. Both are in some sense outsiders to the communities that persecute them: Joe is a stranger passing through, and Eddie has a prison record, though he is attempting to go straight. Both are perceived as marginal persons and are thus ideal candidates for scapegoating. Neither is tried for the crime of which he is accused. And both are loved and inspired by a strong woman.

IDENTIFICATIONS CREATE PERSPECTIVES.

Narrative films use a host of cinematic, musical, and dramatic techniques to cue our identifications. Directors use these to elicit the audience responses that they hope to achieve.

Because Lang was an expressionist filmmaker, the cues in *Fury* are all there, from shadows to smiles, and the contrasts are striking. Several endearing scenes with Joe and Katherine occur before his ordeal in the town, firmly establishing our positive identifications with them. In stark contrast, the townspeople are depicted as a tinderbox of self-righteousness, slander, and malice.

Unlike classic murder mysteries, *Fury* is not an actual scapegoating *event*—namely, a sacrificial ritual in which the audience participates through its identifications with persecutors who see themselves as blameless. *Fury* tells Joe's and Katherine's story from their own perspective, not that of the persecutory mob. Like *M*, it is a story *about* scapegoating. The Hebrew scriptures, with which Lang would have been familiar since childhood, contain many such meta-sacrificial stories revealing the innocence of the victim. Their culmination and clearest expression occur in the foundational event of Christianity—the Passion of Christ.

Fury is a profoundly but inconsistently anti-sacrificial story that offers closure through a just assignment of guilt without violent consequences. The guilty are left to stew in their shame. If we take pleasure in that expectation, our needs for catharsis are then satisfied.

You Only Live Once is also anti-sacrificial insofar as it cues us to identify with the two victims. But Eddie's innocence is compromised by his criminal record and his killing of the chaplain. However, the community that first stigmatizes and then pursues and kills him and Joan without due process of law displays the same cruelty that we see in the mob that attempts to kill Joe.

To achieve closure, the film must end with Eddie's and Joan's deaths. They mustn't succeed in crossing the border into Canada, for most audiences are realistic enough to know that the couple's troubles wouldn't have ended there.

You Only Live Once is a romantic tragedy carefully crafted to enable catharsis without the transfer of guilt that is achieved in lesser films through violent expulsion of a perceived and "othered" evil-doer. The story's "community"—the townspeople as well as the state apparatus that pursues and punishes Eddie—is mixed in its culpability for Eddie's and Joan's deaths, so we cannot identify any single "block" of persecutors like the one in *Fury*. Here, the persecutions are not a focus but a foil for focus on Eddie's and Joan's dilemma in resisting them.

Once the appropriate identifications are in place, we will unconsciously mimic the couple's emotions, from love and hope to fear and desperation—and we will vicariously experience the sting of injustice that dooms them. We will leave the scene feeling sad rather than triumphant.

The Woman in the Window (1944)

This film and Lang's next one (*Scarlet Street*, 1945), both use the talents of Edward G. Robinson, Joan Bennett, and Dan Duryea to tell the story of a respectable middle-aged man who is seduced by the siren song of a *femme fatale* and becomes involved in shady dealings and murder.

In this film, Robinson is Richard Wanley, a psychology professor, husband, and father. When his wife leaves on a holiday with the children, Wanley's thoughts begin to wander. First, he notices a painting displayed in the window of a gallery adjoining his club. It is the portrait of a beautiful and sensuous woman named Alice Reed (Joan Bennett). He gazes at it for a long time before entering the club. Inside, he sits reading in a comfortable leather-bound winged armchair with a nightcap on the side-table. He falls asleep while reading the highly erotic *Song of Solomon*, which he has found in the club's library. When he awakens, he leaves the gallery and returns once more to gaze at the portrait.

Alice happens to walk by and discovers him admiring the portrait. They chat. She invites him to join her somewhere for a drink, after which she invites him to her apartment. Shortly after they reach there, her wealthy clandestine lover, Claude Mazard, bursts in unexpectedly and attacks Wanley. Alice hands Wanley some scissors with which to defend himself, and Wanley kills Mazard.

Though Wanley has acted in self-defense, he knows that the scandal will ruin his marriage and his career. He and Alice conspire to cover up the incident, and he disposes of Mazard's body off a country road, unwittingly leaving several clues behind. The body is discovered and the authorities offer a $10,000 reward to anyone who can lead them to the killer.

Mazard's body-guard, Heidt (Dan Duryea)—a person without nuance—learns of his boss's death and the proffered reward. Figuring that Alice must be involved, he attempts to blackmail her. The next day, Wanley advises her to poison him with an overdose of a prescription drug that he has obtained. When Heidt returns to her for his first payment, he is suspicious of the drink she has offered him, leaves it untasted, and departs with the payment. She immediately phones Wanley at his club to inform him that she has failed, and Wanley then pours the remaining portion of the drug into his own drink.

As Heidt is leaving Alice's apartment, he is confronted by the police, who believe him to be the killer. Heidt dies in a shoot-out with them. Alice phones Wanley again to tell him the news, but he doesn't pick up the phone. He has died from the overdose.

At this point there is what is known in film-making as a "match cut," similar to the one that occurs at the end of *The Wizard of Oz*, where Dorothy wakes up to realize her adventures have only been a dream. Wanley has dozed off in his armchair while reading *The Song of Solomon*. As he leaves the club, he is relieved to find "Mazard" at the coat-check desk and "Heidt," the doorman, saluting him on the way out.

He stops briefly in front of the gallery window where Alice's portrait is displayed and gazes at it again. A streetwalker approaches him with an offer, to which he reacts by running away, presumably back to his family.

The Woman in the Window is a fever-dream of guilt brought on by a convergence of lust and conscience. Wanley's situation, exacerbated by his ineptitude and Alice's, starts out badly and gets steadily worse. Everything goes wrong, leaving Wanley feeling like a hunted man who is finally cornered after entering a *cul-de-sac* of his own making.

The fact that we can feel Wanley's panic and desperation means that (1) we've identified with him despite all his flawed decisions and that (2) our catharsis is underway.

M's Hans Beckert was both a murderer and a victim. Wanley's dream-double, however, is, if anything, just a hapless fool. And yet, Lang prompts us to identify with both of them by showing us their humanness. In Beckert's case, we know that compulsions to murder children are signs of severe—but perhaps treatable— mental disorder. As for Wanley, we know (don't we?) that anyone is capable of impulsive behavior that can end in disgrace. Nevertheless, our initial identification with him becomes strained as we witness his descent into the underworld.

But Lang's film does not show us Heidt's human side or channel any of our empathy in his direction. Lang knows that his film audience will breathe a sigh of relief when Heidt is killed in the film's climax. What, after all, is a *film noir* without a catharsis—in this case, the purging of all the negative feelings (fear, anxiety, guilt, etc.) that it has aroused in us? Heidt's death certainly contributes to this catharsis by removing a major obstacle to the success of Wanley's plan, but by that time, there is little doubt that Wanley's plan is to circumvent responsibility for what he has both done and attempted to do.

Wanley's suicide is the main cathartic event and, significantly, it occurs almost simultaneously with Heidt's, delivering an uninterrupted release of tension. Most audiences will have shared Wanley's despair and felt relieved that he is finally liberated from it.

The Woman in the Window is vestigially sacrificial. Functionally, from the audience's point of view, the sacrificial victim is always the one whom everyone can agree is not just foolish or mentally disturbed but consistently malign. Though "malign" would certainly describe Heidt, he is peripheral to Wanley, a much more complex character who seems destined for sacrifice but is *not* malign.

I would characterize this film as mostly anti-sacrificial. It interrupts and undermines a sacrifice in progress (Wanley's capture and expulsion) by fostering a partially positive identification with the victim. For those who insist on an immolation, there is always Heidt.

Scarlet Street (1945)

In Fritz Lang's *Scarlet Street*, a pair of con artists (Kitty and Charlie, played by Joan Bennett and Dan Duryea) and their dupe (Chris / Edward G. Robinson) become the story's *functional* scapegoats—like Heidt in *The Woman in the Window* and Harry in *Blue Gardenia* (see below).

Kitty is murdered, and her partner, Charlie, is found guilty of the crime and executed.

But Charlie did not kill Kitty. He only found her dead and then clumsily left evidence of his presence at the scene. Complicating matters for him, he was not in good standing with the police.

The murderer is Chris, a bank employee whose hobby is painting and whose harridan wife keeps telling him he can't paint. Middle-aged and never having experienced love, he has believed the beautiful Kitty's professions of love for him. He spends his savings setting her up, then embezzles money from his employer to satisfy her escalating demands. Meanwhile, Charlie has been purloining Chris's paintings and attempting to sell them. One of the galleries offers top dollar for them and wants to know the artist's name. Charlie names Kitty. She soon becomes the new darling of the art world, and money started pouring in—all without Chris's knowledge.

Until Chris discovers his paintings in a gallery with Kitty's signature on them, he is blind to the signs that he is being played. When the scales do finally fall from his eyes, he confronts Kitty, who cruelly taunts him for having believed that she could ever marry a pitiful man like him. Chris's hand falls upon an ice-pick, which he uses to kill her.

But all the evidence points to Charlie, who realizes what has happened but cannot convince the police or, later, the jurors, that Chris has murdered Kitty out of revenge for stealing his paintings.

Chris is asked to testify at Charlie's trial and denies knowing how to paint–which is in fact what his wife had always told him. To identify himself as the painter would implicate him in the crime. He lets Charlie take the rap, and Charlie is later executed.

Chris seems to feel no remorse at first, but then a brief conversation with a fellow train traveler—a crime reporter, in fact—stirs his conscience. The man opines that no one ever gets away with murder, for even if the law doesn't punish the murderer, hisr conscience forever will. Chris does not believe him at first but, returning home, he begins hallucinating, hearing Kitty's voice taunting him and declaring her love for Charlie—a "real man." He cannot sleep. He cannot still his conscience. He tries to hang himself but is rescued by neighbors.

Though his employer has not pressed charges against Chris over the embezzlement, Chris's reputation is ruined and he becomes a derelict. One night, two officers find him sleeping on a bench in Central Park and tell him to move on. As he walks away, one of the officers remarks to the other, "He's got a crazy idea he killed a couple of people five or six years ago. Can't get it out of his mind. Always trying to give himself up. Wants to be tried and executed. *You* know these nuts!"

Scarlet Street is unusual for its absence of sympathetic foreground characters. The three principals are all guilty—Chris more than the two others, despite their swindling—and all three carry our guilt away with them—one as a murder victim, one as an executee of the state, and the third as a derelict, expelled by society into the streets of New York City.

The functional similarity between "primitive" ritual human sacrifice and modern state executions suggests historical continuity. Both aim to put a cap on violence by means of violence itself—a violence that will always have the last word because it is the only form of violence that God or the sovereign state will allow. Their monopoly on violence is perfectly demonstrated in a sacrificial act of murder—a murder that is sacralized by priests and prison chaplains so that it may be permitted to happen despite deeply-rooted societal prohibitions against murder. In fact, it will never even be called "murder." It is described as the "punishment" of a person held responsible for the community's troubles.

Is this all a conspiracy? No, and it's not by design. It's a reflex built into the fabric of what makes us human. All states and all religions operate in this way, for both depend for their existence on a unanimous belief in their transcendent authority—an authority that is exempt from the prohibitions that apply to immanent human beings.

Capital punishment as we know it is itself a sacrificial ritual conducted by a community (in this case, the state) to rid itself of a perceived troublemaker. When it serves as the stated or implied conclusion to a murder mystery, its efficacy depends on our identification with the society that has authorized the execution. It would be hard to imagine any other plot device that could bring us this close to participation in what we so clearly recognize in other settings as ritual violence by a majority against a minority.

Finally, Lang's script makes it clear that Chris is initially impenitant about murdering Kitty and allowing Charlie to take the rap. We are not told what rationalizations he has devised, but there comes a moment of recognition—or perhaps a "conversion" in the style of Paul the Apostle—when the fellow traveler (the voice of God?) reminds him that he has a conscience. This is his sentence—to be tormented by his conscience until he dies. His burden of guilt can never be lifted, and he is forever an outsider, a wanderer in the streets of the city.

We are perhaps meant to feel satisfied that justice has been done, even at the price of knowing that Charlie has been executed for a murder he did not commit, and that Kitty should have been brought to justice and not brutally murdered. But the instrument of their deaths is not the state, but Chris, who is never brought to justice. This might indicate a failure of closure, but instead, closure is achieved through the activation of Chris's conscience, his permanent expulsion from ordered society, and the hopelessness to which he is doomed.

There must be unanimity, and loose ends must all be neatly clipped and swept away. To be troubled by the outcome is to break the identification–another way of breaking the faith, for faith is unanimity.

The Blue Gardenia (1953)

In *The Blue Gardenia*, Lang adapts a story by Vera Caspary illustrating one of the many ways that the sacrificial trajectory can be plotted.

A telephone operator (Nora, played by Anne Baxter) receives a letter from her soldier boyfriend announcing that he has fallen in love with his nurse in the military hospital where he is recovering. In great emotional distress and needing company, Nora accepts a dinner invitation from a man whom everyone else knows to be a philanderer and a cad (Harry, played by Raymond Burr). True to form, Harry plies her with one drink after another until she can barely stand, then gets her into a cab and takes her to his apartment, where he attempts to rape her. Though nearly unconscious by that time, she yet manages to grab a poker from the fireplace and swing it at him before she blacks out.

When she comes to, she finds Harry dead. Panicked and still drunk, she hastily flees his apartment, accidentally leaving a shoe and a handkerchief behind.

At this point, our sympathies are clearly with her, as she has been portrayed as an innocent lamb and Harry as a wolf. We see her consumed by guilt and anxiety, unable to sleep, and terrified that the police are about to find her. She knows that she cannot continue on this way.

A couple of "helpers" appear in the characters of an understanding roommate (Ann Sothern) and a handsome newspaper columnist (Richard Conte) who gains her trust and offers to help her. At this point, a bit of romancing occurs, fortifying our identification with her and her galant defender by drawing upon the natural sympathies that audiences feel for young lovers.

Nevertheless, she is soon captured and prosecuted for the crime.

The writer of the original story wanted her readers to identify with Nora as the innocent victim of a rape attempt who might yet be statutorily guilty of murdering her assailant. This sets readers up to expect that a miscarriage of justice will occur if Nora is punished for the crime.

But this story is not about the justice system, and the writer has not primed us to question its legitimacy. Nor does Lang want us to do so. For the audience, Nora's dilemma is a painful conundrum, raising a perhaps uncomfortable question: Can a woman be punished for killing a man who is trying to rape her?

In sacrificial terms, Nora seems about to become a victim twice over—this time at the hands of the state itself, which may consider attempted rape to be an inadmissable excuse for killing the aggressor. Neither the writer nor the director can allow that to happen, for it would raise questions of social justice and make dramatic closure impossible. So they introduce a *deus ex machina* in the form of a peripheral character, seen briefly at the beginning of the film—who comes forward and confesses to the crime. We learn that she is a spurned lover who came to Harry's apartment shortly after Nora passed out in front of the fireplace. Finding the scented handkerchief that Nora had dropped in the kitchen, she was overcome by jealous rage, grabbed the poker from Harry's hand and killed him with it.

The function of the scapegoat, both in spontaneous mob violence and in sacrificial ritual, is to carry away the collective guilt of the community. The only way for this plot to satisfy our need for catharsis is for Harry to be portrayed as so obviously odious that we welcome his death. Within the imaginative frame of the story, we cannot picture him as a scapegoat, for he is hardly innocent. And the story is not *about* scapegoating as Lang's earlier film *Fury* (1936) so clearly is. Nevertheless, some part of our brain is happy that Harry is dead, because our collective animus has focused on him and him alone. Thus, he *functions* as a scapegoat for us, the audience, even if he is not one within the frame of the story.

In a murder mystery, there are two communities—one onstage and one off. If Nora had been found guilty and punished, we, the offstage audience, would not normally have agreed with the part of the onstage audience that is represented by the justice system of the state. We would instead have identified with Nora and her helpers. This would have fractured the unanimity that the ritual always aims to achieve, and a restoration of social order would have been impossible. A failure of unanimity pollutes the sacrality of the sacrifice.

The real murderess will, of course, be punished, but she will not have the audience's sympathies. Thus, she joins Harry in helping carry away the audience's guilt, rancor, and other unwelcome emotions.

This polarization of blame happens reflexively as rampant conflict within communities becomes reoriented toward one or two individuals. It is tempting to hypothesize that it occurs in all murder mysteries as well as several other genres.

The Big Heat (1953)

In one of Lang's most famous *films noirs*, Glenn Ford is Dave Bannion, a detective in a town whose police commissioner is in cahoots with the local mob boss, Mike Lagana. Bannion despises Lagana and his goons and wants to bring them to justice, but his superiors throw interference his way. When he persists, they confiscate his badge. Undeterred, he pursues a suicide case that is sure to implicate Lagana, but in the course of doing so, four women die, and one of them is his own wife.

Film critic Roger Ebert, reviewing the film in 2004, argues that Bannion is indirectly responsible for the remaining three women's deaths because of his carelessness in handling the case—but that his "carelessness" may have been motivated. His fearless heroism and single-mindedness in taking down the mob ostensibly blind him to the dangers that his tactics pose for these women—all of whom, except his wife, have been mixed up with it. One of the latter, a bar-fly, is found strangled in a roadside ditch after she is overheard disclosing a key bit of evidence to Bannion. When his wife is killed by a car bomb that was intended for him, he seems willing to stop at nothing to avenge her death, and the remaining two women arguably become the instruments of his revenge. At one point, he subtly encourages one of them—Debby, the girlfriend of Lagana's second-in-command, Vince Stone—to murder the other woman, despite the likelihood that the mob will retaliate against her for doing so. She does, they do, and the case is blown wide open.

Like Joe in Lang's earlier film, *Fury* (1936), Bannion is a man fighting a mob. In *Fury*, the mob is the entire community gone rogue, and in *The Big Heat*, it is a corrupt subset of the larger community. Both heroes are persecuted by the mob and seek revenge, but Joe comes to his senses at the last moment, while Bannion does not. For Bannion, the ends—purification and revenge—justify the means, and he is careful enough to stay within the law while pursuing them. If, indeed, Bannion has manipulated three of the women into their own deaths as a way of smoking out the mob, then Ebert was probably right about him.

Bannion's righteous contempt for the mob is matched only by his moral revulsion toward everyone they have corrupted. Though Stone's girlfriend (Gloria Grahame) turns to Bannion for help after Stone has abused her, he makes clear to her that he is not going to touch anything that Stone has touched. When Stone finds out that she has talked to Bannion, he throws boiling coffee in her face and she flees back to Bannion. Now severely disfigured, she is ripe for sacrifice to his interests—"marked" for victim status by her scars.

In scenes with his wife and child, Bannion is portrayed as a patient and forgiving man, but his mindset toward these other three women is punitive. Does he perhaps consider them expendable? Disposable? Tainted?

As usual, I will try to identify plot elements that fulfill the requirements of a sacrificial ritual, which I consider this film to be. They are: identification; clear attribution of innocence and guilt; unanimity; expulsion; and closure. Each element in this set serves two audiences—one real and one virtual—and, within those are sub-audiences reflecting all the ways people process what is represented to them. The offstage audience's differential identifications with the story's characters are key to their experiencing catharsis, which I believe to be the purpose of these dramas. It is the job of the writer and the director to find plot devices and visual cues that will help establish identifications (or transferences) conducive to such a "purging" of the emotions.

In straightforward sacrificial terms, I see Bannion as an impassioned executor serving the uncorrupted part of his community by single-handedly purging the corrupted part. Nothing is left of the festering wound after he cleans it out with surgical thoroughness. Everyone who was associated with the mob is either dead or indicted. In Bannion's world, there are no shades of grey.

Such absolutism may not appeal to everyone, as Roger Ebert's review demonstrates, but it is a key feature of cathartic representations wherever they serve the purposes of sacrificial ritual, for it offers clear delineations between good and evil, unanimity, expulsion, and closure, provided that the intended identifications are in place.

Human Desire (1954)

In Fritz Lang's 1954 film, *Human Desire*, a Korean War veteran (Jeff, played by Glenn Ford) returns home to his job as a train engineer. Well-liked by everyone, he is fond of a childhood friend (Ellen / Kathleen Case) who plainly loves and wants to marry him. Her father is Jeff's co-engineer, and the scene seems to be set for a happy marriage ahead.

Meanwhile, a minor official in the railroad company (Carl / Broderick Crawford) blows his stack with his superior and is fired. He persuades his beautiful wife (Vicki / Gloria Grahame), to visit a shipping company executive (Mr. Owens) who has some clout with the railroad and may be able to get him reinstated. Vicki's mother was once Owens' housekeeper, so Vicki knows him well. In fact, as we later learn, she knows him very well.

Vicki accomplishes her mission, but she is gone for five hours and, upon her return, Carl ascertains from her that she has been with Owen the entire time but not at his office. Consumed by jealousy and rage, he slaps her around and demands that she set Owens up for revenge by writing him a letter offering to meet him on the train to Chicago that very evening. Though Carl drags Vicki along with him in order to get access to

Owens, she offers little resistance. Pushing his way into Owens' compartment behind Vicki, he brutally murders Owens and transfers the letter from Owens' pocket to his own. It is to be his insurance that Vicki won't betray him.

Escaping the scene of a crime is always difficult on a passenger train, and that is perhaps why it is a familiar and effective plot device. It compresses the action into a single narrow corridor only interrupted by vestibules separating the cars. It is impossible to anticipate who will enter from either end.

Coincidentally, Jeff has boarded the train as a passenger and is enjoying a cigarette in the vestibule of the next car. Carl instructs Vicki to distract him, and she has no trouble luring him into his own compartment so that her husband can discreetly leave the scene of the crime. Having already traded on her sex appeal with Owens, Vicki now does so with Jeff, and he falls for her.

But Vicki's gambit is about more than just distracting Jeff, and his hormones are offering her just the opportunity she needs to exploit him. She will give herself to him until he is sure of her love, then persuade him to rid her of Carl forever.

During the inquest following Owens' death, Jeff is asked if he saw anyone coming out of the car where Owens was killed. Jeff looks straight at Vicki and answers, "No."

Jeff has previously been presented as a good-hearted and honest man, but life is testing him. We are hoping he will wake up to the moral issues he is facing. Like Chris in *Scarlet Street*, he is blinded by passion.

Vicki leads him on until she thinks the time is right. She then tells him the truth about what happened on the train and about the letter that Carl carries on his body. She subtly proposes that he kill Carl in the freight yard later that night. At that moment, Jeff's expression becomes very serious and we can almost hear the gears meshing in his head as he looks at her and truly sees her for the first time. Then he leaves.

Hours later, Jeff returns, saying that Carl had been so drunk that he pitied him and spared his life. He tosses the letter on the table and laments that she had almost succeeded in corrupting him, pulling him into the seedy world that she inhabits. Then he walks out.

The next day, Vicki walks out on Carl and boards the train for the city. But, just as the train is leaving the station, Carl suddenly enters her compartment, begs her to return, and promises to mend his ways. When she rebuffs and taunts him, he becomes hostile and reminds her about the letter. But when he reaches into his coat pocket for it, it isn't there. She laughs in his face, describes her revulsion toward him, and brags that she almost persuaded Jeff to murder him. For Carl, this is one blow too many, for he loses every vestige of self-control and kills her.

As this is happening, Jeff is busy engineering both the train and his next move, which will be to ask Ellen to accompany him to a dance. He smiles as he toots the train's horn.

Lang's film ends there, and we may be left wondering what will become of Carl and whether he might seek revenge against Jeff as he did earlier against Owens. In the final shot, it's only Jeff's happy smile that assures us that the matter is, for all practical purposes, closed.

In attempting to identify the sacrificial aspects of this story, I begin by asking, "Whose expulsion delivers the cathartic effects that we expect? In successful mysteries, more than one individual may be killed, but the audience will identify only with the ones they believe to be innocent. So which character or characters carry away our collective guilt?

Clearly, Carl and Vicki do, provided that Carl doesn't escape. Jeff comes perilously close to going down with them but steps back from the brink just in time.

Chapter 6: Styles of Impersonation

All the world's a stage,
And all the men and women merely players;
They have their exits and their entrances;
And one man in his time plays many parts,
His acts being seven ages. ...

William Shakespeare, *As You Like It*

Shakespeare's iconographic characterizations of the seven ages in the rest of this speech reveal an important intuition about the universality of mimesis and its role in the formation of the self. His plays are evidence of his preoccupation with this theme and have, in fact, been a rich vein of insight for scholars writing about mimesis. His genius was to explore this intuition theatrically and poetically in a manner that could be understood by any man or woman.

Impersonation is a performative representation of another's self, made possible by mimesis. Given that the self is a dynamic multiplicity of other selves, we are all impersonators, though most of us are unconscious of being so. The dramatic actor is simply a skilled impersonator who consciously controls his characterizations in order to create a temporary and partial illusion. Yes, we know, even as we watch a Harry

Potter movie, that we're watching a performance by Daniel Radcliffe.

Impersonations are also used offstage for purposes of deceit, which can only succeed when the impersonator creates an illusion so total that it may even deceive himrself. Remaining permanently or semi-permanently in character lessens the chances of exposure but also carries the risk of a psychological doubling, in which the subject can no longer distinguish between hisr self and a particular other self. The self of the particular other then shadows or overshadows the subject's already multitudinous self, resulting in either compartmentalization (as we'll see in *The Reader*) or annexation, where the subject truly believes that he is Napoleon.

Sometimes doubling *precedes* or accompanies the subject's deceit, as in Patricia Highsmith's psychological thriller, *The Talented Mr. Ripley* (1955), adapted for the screen in 1999 and starring Matt Damon as Ripley. Ripley deceives others in order to protect his obsessive identification with Dickie Greenleaf (Jude Law), a wealthy and charming playboy. Ripley desires to possess Dickie, to appropriate his very identity—to annex Dickie's self into his own—to *become* Dickie. But Dickie's charm turns to contempt when he sees Ripley's obsession for what it. Ripley, having imitated Dickie's regard, now imitates his contempt and turns it first of all against himself. To forestall narcissistic deflation, Ripley turns on Dickie and bludgeons him to death with an oar. His identification with Dickie can now proceed unimpeded by Dickie's obstruction of it.

Transparent Impersonations in Satirical Skits

I hope it is clear by now that my use of the term "sacrificial rites" is very broad and runs the gamut from Punch and Judy shows to blood sacrifice. Comic impersonation is simply at the lighter end of the gamut.

Serial comedic impersonators such as the cast of *Saturday Night Live* have wardrobes full of personalities modeled on those of particular well-known individuals such as celebrities and political figures—or on character types such as floozies, nosy landladies, and bungling detectives. This is also true of actors in general, but when we see a comedic impersonator cycling through personalities from one skit to another, while caricaturing each one, we are less likely to forget that she is not the characters that she impersonates. Nor does she want us to forget that.

The comedic impersonator creates an illusion while simultaneously framing it as one, thereby interrupting *our* identifications with the characters that she depicts. *Her* success, however, depends on her ability to identify with her models while holding them at at arm's length. Her impressions of them are like the costumes that she returns to the wardrobe after the show. She never allows the self of the other—the impersonated model—to either subsume or eclipse her own.

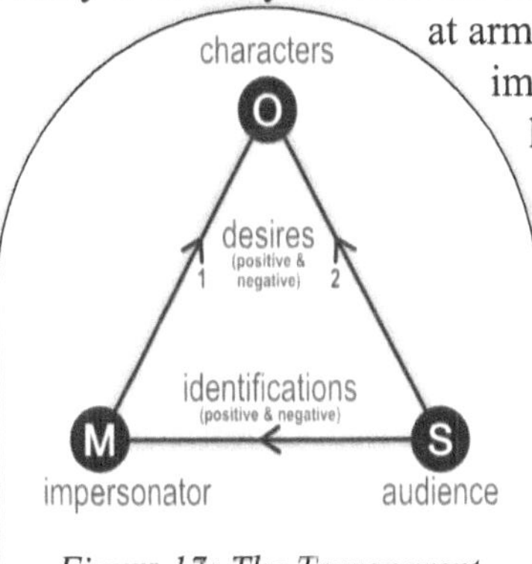

Figure 17: The Transparent Impersonations of Comic Skits

If she blocks our identifications with her characters, she nonetheless needs us—her audience—to identify with *her*, for she is to model for us her particular regard for the character she is impersonating. Why? To make us "other" himr through laughter. The character becomes the object of ridicule—the scapegoat in this cathartic ritual. It's not Carol Burnett you're laughing at. It's her characters.

None of this is to say that the Carol Burnett Show was simply a cover for pagan blood rites or a pretext for malice and cruelty. Her skits were both funny and inoffensive, for she was far more interested in parodying certain character types, or traits, than the individuals who embodied them. Her slapstick interpretations of Norma Desmond's narcissism were harmless because Desmond was a purely fictional character representing the narcissism that both enables and afflicts Hollywood celebrities. They may deserve to be pitied rather than pilloried, and our laughter may arguably be cruel, but at least Burnett's parodies of them are never likely to incur reprisals or contribute to social fracturing. Additionally, the narcissists in her audience are given a space to "other" their own narcissism, a process of guilt-shifting that enables catharsis, as I discussed in Chapter 3 ("Scapegoating").

Isn't this the point of parody, ridicule, and satire? There may be a bit of Norma Desmond in all of us, and we're only too happy to laugh at someone more narcissistic than ourselves.

Like many farcical impersonators, Carol Burnett occasionally "breaks the frame" of her skits by erupting into seemingly spontaneous laughter at her own or another's lines. This is pure modeling. It guides us through a cathartic experience of laughing *with* her *at* an object that she has chosen for the purpose. That object is usually a character type whom the audience may "safely" subject to ridicule in a transfer of guilt without blowback. (See Chapter 3).

Impersonation makes no bones about what it is, but it tells us a lot about who we are.

The impersonator stages for us a certain wisdom about the composition of the self—that it is always and only an *assemblage* of other selves that are themselves multiplicities of other selves. None is autonomous. All are linked through mimesis. The serial impersonator is able to consciously call out the parallel impersonations the rest of us unconsciously perform every day.

Drag

The art form known as "drag" may be practiced by anyone, whether straight or gay, male or female. The practitioners are called "drag queens," regardless of their gender identifications, though those identifying as males are the most common.

All drag queens performatively impersonate a glamorous woman (never a man) whose gender signifiers (as expressed in mannerisms, physical attributes, and voice) are already not just salient but exaggerated—for example, the Mae Wests and Marilyn Monroes—and then they dial up the exaggeration, but gently, because over-exaggeration may distort the image beyond recognition.

Many entertainers have excelled in impersonations of glamorous women, but not all of them have billed themselves as "drag queens," either because drag is only part of what they do onstage or their audiences are not ready to make the connection. Carol Burnett, despite her impersonations of Norma Desmond, Queen Elizabeth I, and Mae West, never encouraged her audiences to think of her as a drag queen, and yet that's what she was, in addition to so much more.

Famous entertainers who *have* billed themselves as drag queens include women like Margot Minelli and men like Jim Bailey and Charles Pierce. The glamorous women they impersonated included Carol Channing, Barbara Streisand, Marlene Dietrich, as well as the ones mentioned earlier.

Opaque Impersonations in Plays and Films

In all of the movies that I have so far discussed, the actors perform impersonations that do not draw attention to themselves in the way that transparent impersonations do. They want us to forget that they are actors, or at least to suspend that knowledge. They veil themselves in their personas so as to *allow* audience identifications with the represented characters rather than themselves, because identifications allow audiences to experience catharsis, without which dramatic narrative fails. Within the narrative frame, the actor must never be seen out of costume, though s/he may play several roles within a single drama. The multiple roles performed by Meryl Streep and Emma Thompson in the film version of Tony Kushner's *Angels in America* are impersonations of this second type insofar as they encourage audience identifications with their characters.

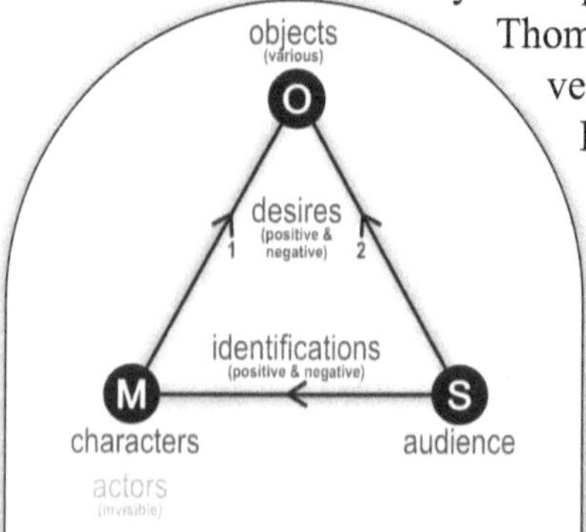

Figure 18: The Opaque Impersonations of Plays and Films

Some method actors have been

known to carry their own identifications too far. When this happens, the boundary between the actor's own self and that of hisr model is weakened, sometimes to the point that s/he cannot easily step out of the model's character after portraying it. Colin Firth had a slight stutter for months after his performance in *The King's Speech*. Such over-identifications are similar in many ways to doubling, which entails the subject's inability to distinguish himrself from the Other.

Audiences may also sometimes over-identify, forgetting the presence of the actor-intermediary. The characters then become so real to them that the proscenium arch cannot hold and they invade the stage to string up the villain of the piece. Historically, this has only happened in cases where the audience had no prior experience of theatrical performance. But it is not uncommon for individual spectators to so totally lose sight of the performer that they believe the character is real. In practice, this means mistaking the actor for the character. If the character is charming, then charm is what the spectator expects to see in the actor should their paths ever cross.

Doubling: Real-life Impersonations that are Opaque to the Impersonator

Besides serial and parallel impersonations, there are relatively fixed, static ones that may remain opaque because they so completely eclipse all the others either all the time or in the presence of a particular model. In these, the subject's/impersonator's identification with the model(s) is strong and perhaps even psychologically and socially problematic. "Doubling," as I described it earlier, is said to account for wartime atrocities committed by normally compassionate individuals. In many cases, these persecutions are modeled by superior officers or the culture at large, and the subject's self is captured and held by the desires of those other selves. Psychological trauma often sets in when the other self withdraws, as depicted in *The Reader*, a 1995 novel by Bernhard Schlink, adapted for the screen in 2008 and starring Kate Winslet as Hanna Schmitz, a Nazi concentration camp guard tried years later for war crimes. In 1963, experimental psychologist Stanley Milgram published a now-famous study of cruelty modeled by authority figures for individuals subject to their mimetic influence.

Satire

Mimetic theory allows us to discover the fundamental unity of all forms of satire. Satire is a sacrificial ritual performed solely at the level of symbolism and representation, without bloodshed, and specializing in cathartic expulsion through derisive laughter.

Satire comes in three basic styles, known as Horatian, Juvenalian, and Menippean. Burnett's farcical satire is Horatian insofar as it evokes laughter mostly without negativity and blame, and with only a *soupçon* of victimization. She does not target individuals, social norms or political, religious, and philosophical beliefs.

The element of cruelty is more salient in Juvenalian satire, which is used to attack political and ideological rivals—individuals, entities, and movements—in order to influence public opinion against them. It is often dark and bitter rather than funny. George Orwell's *1984* and *Animal Farm* are Juvenalian, as is Nabokov's *Lolita,* Stanley Kubrick's *Dr. Strangelove*, and Joseph Heller's *Catch-22.* Juvenalian satire can be very divisive, exacerbating social tensions between audiences. The benefits of catharsis and social ordering are then felt only among those laughing. The rest are plotting their revenge.

Menippean satire lies somewhere between the two others. It is more judgmental than the Horatian variety but less aggressive than the Juvenalian. It targets human foibles rather than specific individuals or their misdeeds. Notable examples from literature are Lewis Carroll's *Alice in Wonderland*, Voltaire's *Candide*, and Jonathan Swift's *Gulliver's Travels*.

Styles of Othering

It may seem preposterous to suggest that styles of othering lie on a continuum that runs from Heinrich Himmler to Carol Burnett and from gladiatorial games to American football. However, the mimetic model takes us beyond appearances right into the neurological functioning of the rational, emotive, and mimetic brains, where we find a single mechanism generating and governing a vast multiplicity of cultural expressions, from human sacrifice to sports, religion, drama, comedy, and political campaigning. Scapegoating never wants to be seen for what it is. It is always remembered as something else—a parody, a contest, a game, a disciplinary action, all of which involve an expulsion preceded by symmetrical conflict.

When the conflict is staged, the real action is always in the audience itself. The day's stresses of conflictual desire are channeled via representation toward a fictional character who has the power to relieve them. That character is the scapegoat, a worthy target for our laughter, derision, and even more violent impulses. S/he is a proxy for some or all of those with whom we are wedged in mundane, everyday conflicts. Laughter breaks up the tension brought about by near-universal prohibitions against laughing derisively in another person's face. Derisive laughter is to be directed only at those who are absent or whom one wishes to provoke.

Poison as Cure

The role of the comedic impersonator is to furnish a target at whom *everyone* (at least in hisr targeted audience) can laugh without fear of reprisals. This amounts to using laughter to cure laughter, and it is analogous to the millennia-old practice of using a poison as a cure—both literally and figuratively. Toxins and venoms have been used to treat ailments since the practice of medicine began. A virus's own DNA is used to combat the virus itself. Wildfires are often contained with controlled burns. Cities are firebombed to end wars. Boys are sent off to war. All sacrificial violence is used as a cure for a larger, more pervasive violence.

The Greek word *pharmakos* refers to an outsider who is sacrificed, i.e, a scapegoat. But it is related to other Greek words like *pharmakeia*, *pharmakon*, and *pharmakeus*, all of which have to do with medicine.

From Symmetrical to Hierarchical Violence

The very survival of our species has always been threatened by our unique capacity for non-instinctual conflict, driven solely by metaphysical desires mirrored betweeen individuals who cannot share a desired object. This is not the territorial sparring of wildebeests, and it is not mere aggression. It occurs in the symbolic realm of interdividuality and representation, where each individual's mirror neurons are activated by the perceived desires of the other. When they look at each other, they see themselves, and that sets them against each other. Social order depends on difference, not identity. As rivals, they are too closely identified and must establish difference (hierarchical ranking) between them while not loosening their grips on the desired object. Some form of violence—physical, verbal, reputational—is sure to ensue and will immediately establish a hierarchy between them.

Symmetrical mirroring creates feedback loops and chain reactions amplifying the emotions driving conflict. When symmetrical rivalries escalate and spread contagiously throughout an entire community, that community cannot come together for collective, cooperative efforts. At some point, *as if providentially*, someone appears, or is found, who can be the focus of everyone's animosity and be blamed for everything.

Mimesis has made us what we are, with all our glories and faults. Our capacity for sharing useful knowledge with other members of our species is unique because it depends on the rational and mimetic brains, which are scarcely detectable in some species and embryonic in others. But these two highly-developed brains have also given us an outsize capacity for negative mimesis expressed as envy, jealousy, malice, slander, and cruelty.

Adversaries are equals, and therefore in tension, until one of them prevails. Then they enter into a hierarchical relationship, where the loser defers to the winner. A whole society engaged in symmetrical conflict can only continue to exist if it re-orders itself into a hierarchy of rights and responsibilities that is periodically renewed through sacrificial rituals of expulsion. This is all very fine for the community minus the victim(s). But it is a flawed solution because the sacrifice must be staged whether or not the victim is in any way guilty for the disturbances. Someone must be found to fill that role—a stranger, a cripple, or perhaps someone already set aside and cultivated for that purpose. As Girard says, a king is a victim with a suspended sentence.

The Metaphysical Nature of Human Desire

To reiterate a point I made earlier, desire—in the restrictive sense that Girard uses it—is not the same as needs and appetites. Only humans experience it to any significant degree. Desire is always modeled on another desire, linking subjects and models in elaborate lattices of interdividuality where their proximity and their symmetry produce conflict and call for hierarchical differentiation. This will be achieved when one of the rivals expels the other from the space of interdividuality and indifferentiation, but that expulsion must be carried out ritualistically—i.e., according to prescribed rules—in order to prevent contamination and contagion. Thus, we have rules governing human activities of every variety, from poker to international relations and from sports competitions to sex. Wherever there is potential for conflict, there are rules for shaping, containing, and channeling it ritualistically. A poker game *is* a ritual. A meeting between heads of state *is* a ritual.

Application of the Cure

Given the autonomous functioning of the brain's mimetic apparatus, metaphysical conflict appears to be an inescapable feature of the human condition. The solution may not be to renounce all desire but rather to avoid being drawn into conflict over it. Our species' success in this so far has hardly been spectacular, but there have been signs of improvement since the earliest times, as cognitive psychologist, linguist, and popular science writer Stephen Pinker has documented in *The Better Angels of Our Nature* (2011) and *Enlightenment Now* (2018).

Imagine an entire community beset by symmetrical conflict that oversteps (violates) the rules and can no longer be shaped, nor contained, nor channeled by them within the space of law (which is the space of rules). When everyone is about to become an outlaw, it's a sign of social disintegration, for societies cannot cohere without respect for their own laws.

A community beset by such levels of internecine conflict will spontaneously apply the imperfect cure to which I've already referred. The imperfect cure is provided by the same second-and-third unconscious brains that gave us the negative consequences of mimetic behavior. It is the *pharmakos* that I previously mentioned—the poison that is also a cure, violence capping violence, the war to ends all wars.

POLARIZATION AS A MIMETIC PHENOMENON

Individuals A and B are rivals, imitating each other's desire for an unsharable object. Individual B has a positive rapport with individual C and models for him his animus toward A. C is susceptible to B's influence, C copies B's animus toward A, and at that instant, the conflict becomes asymmetrical, which is to say, hierarchical, for one of the rivals now has an ally.

From that point, the allies have a greater attractive mass than their opponent and can draw in more allies. Soon an angry crowd forms around individual A, and A is eliminated. The crowd has become united in a common purpose, and the crisis brought about by symmetrical conflict has ended.

I have discussed certain implications of this transformation elsewhere in this book. If everyone in a community can be drawn into the crowd, its polarization against individual A will be remembered as a cure for the symmetrical violence that was destroying the polis. The community will then want to periodically re-apply the cure to head off or stanch the symmetrical violence of all against all. Re-enactment will be performed through whatever means are customary, from state executions to cinematic representations thereof, from the casual chess game to the high-stakes chess tournament. The cathartic effects of these repetitions will vary widely in form and intensity, but their aim will always be the same—to replace symmetrical conflict with a more stable hierarchical order.

Chapter 7: Pathologies

Freudian vs. Mimetic Conceptions of the Ego

Freud's theories of ego and superego formation foreshadowed mimetic theory's triangular model of self, other (model, rival, or obstacle), and object. In the mimetic model, the ego is the self (subject), and the superego is the model, rival, and obstacle all rolled into one. It's not hard to see why Freud, a respected member of Austria's patriarchal society, saw a father-son relationship inscribed in this: The father models his desire for the mother; the son imitates the father's desire; and the father then reminds him who is older, stronger, and better connected. This is all done spontaneously

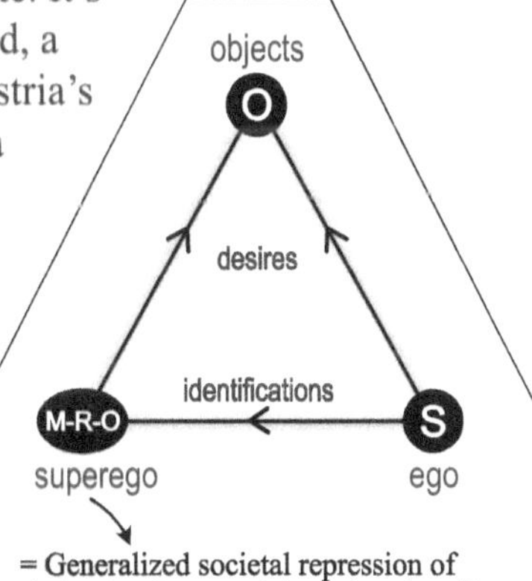

Figure 19: Ego and Superego

185

in everyday matters or ritually in the presence of other elders.

Freud recognized that a child's ego is not formed until s/he can objectify himrself. Jacques Lacan called this process the "mirror stage" of development, where the "mirror" reflects the subject's image in the eyes of others. During this stage, the subject acquires a sense of himrself as separate—an object of others' gaze—and s/he becomes a self—an object of hisr own gaze. This is the ego—the sense of who "I" am—and it requires careful cultivation by parents and others who influence the child.

What Freud did not appear to recognize was that the self-objectification occurring in the mirror stage is a mimetic process in which the subject's self comes into being relationally, through imitation of another's desires. The onset of mimetic desire with all its attendant rivalries is also the moment when the self—the ego—is formed.

The ego is not, as Freud believed, a separate entity. Instead, it is a composite identity forged in the interdividual rapport, that area of overlap between one individual's mimetic "brain" and another's (See Chapter 1). The subject's self is shaped by other selves perceived as models, rivals, or obstacles. Its needs and appetites are its own, but its desires are not.

The self comes into being when it first imitates another's desire and then unconsciously claims that desire as its own, denying its own susceptibility and the other's influence. Misrecognition is key to the third brain's strategy in forming the self, which, as a type of holon, is integral even while functioning as part of a larger system. The self is a complex nexus of influences, but it is also a unit of social functioning responsible for its own processing of sensory data. It must be careful about blaming other units when its output is less than expected. It's all about accountability.

The desires that form the self may be expressed either positively or negatively along the entire spectrum of beliefs, thoughts, opinions, and behaviors. The subject wants X because the model wants it, or the subject rejects X because the model has rejected it. The model may also reject the subject's claims to ownership of the object, in which case the subject may respond mimetically by rejecting the model's claims, at which point the two becomes rivals.

The subject's conviction that hisr desires are unique and that s/he is their sole proprietor is simply a cherished and statistically normal illusion, but it is not a place of wisdom, which always requires recognition of reality.

The Superego and the Alter Ego: Initiation vs. Resistance

The second developmental stage that Freud identified involves the formation of a superego, a sense of oneself as a social being who cannot survive on hisr own, i.e., without entry into the social order, which is governed by whatever body of law or custom—sacred or secular—prevails in the community. Ideally, this stage begins with an initiation or coming-of-age ceremony during which the initiate's place in the community is secured through formal submission to its obligations and prohibitions.

Initiates who are ambivalent about this requirement may become openly rebellious and/or deceitful, but eventually, most achieve some degree of equilibrium, provided that the community itself is not in disarray.

A less desirable solution for the reluctant initiate is to unconsciously split off and sequester a part of himrself in the form of an alter ego. This may be both necessary and advantageous for the children of abusive parents or for people living under oppressive regimes, but it is foolish when the laws and customs of the community are just and necessary. The task of the conscious brain is to discern, over time and through experience, the difference between justice and injustice. When the conscious, rational brain is unprepared or ill-equipped to do this, it continues providing rationales and justifications for what the emotive and mimetic brains want.

What any society—just or unjust—requires of its members is submission to a set of prohibitions and obligations—in short, all the things one must or must not do. Participation in rituals is required, while incest is forbidden. One must not lie, cheat, steal or murder.

Sequestration is taboo because it is duplicitous. The individual who breaks off and sequesters a part of himrself cannot be trusted. S/he has held something back, and whatever it is, it must be asocial, for otherwise there would be no reason to conceal it. The self belongs to the community and should be under community control. So says the community council.

Sequestration in Dorian Gray

The Picture of Dorian Gray, which I reviewed earlier, is about a man who has closeted a part of himself out of fear of social death. The closeted part—his alter ego—violates taboos that restrict his pleasure and constrain his cruelty. The story brings to mind the real-life dilemma of its author, a homosexual living in 19th-century Britain, where "buggery," as they called it, was punishable by 10 years imprisonment. My own autobiography, *Gay Revelations* (2021), is about the self-fragmentation that I experienced for decades as a closeted gay man.

The choice between sequestration and social death is painful at any stage of life. During adolescence, the superego is in a developmental stage involving continuous negotiations with the ego. But patterns of refusal and accommodation established that early in life are not always informed by sound judgment, so the negotiations continue. Life-long sequestration, whether in response to just laws or unjust ones, is hardly an ideal outcome for either an individual or hisr community, as duplicity does in fact have negative psychosocial consequences. The sequestered alter ego cannot easily be held to accounts, which makes it a social liability. Oscar Wilde faced social death after his public exposure and imprisonment. His fictional creation, Dorian Gray, murdered the first man who discovered his secret, then plunged the dagger into his alter ego, as represented by the sequestered portrait—all in an effort to avoid social death. Any lie, any act of cruelty was justified as long as he did not have to face the consequences of his Mephistophelian bargain—for he was by that time so utterly corrupted that no redemption was possible. His ego and alter ego were reunited only in the throes of death.

The Faust Legend

The legend of Faust comes naturally to mind in connection with Dorian Gray's refusal of the superego's prohibitions. Faust's desire for unlimited power, worldly pleasure, and knowledge is so great that he barters his soul to Mephistopheles (the Devil) in order to procure these goods. The beautiful and innocent Gretchen is the principal casualty of his megalomania. However, Faust does not develop an alter ego as Dorian Gray does, for the concept of an internalized Other was not to be fleshed out until nearly three centuries later. His rejection of the traditional prohibitions of Catholicism is in plain sight, as befits a tale told for the moral betterment of the masses.

The Faust legend began in Germany in the 16th century, long before Freud proposed his theory of ego and superego formation. It was intended—and performed—as a cautionary tale not unlike the morality plays that preceded it all throughout Europe. These were popularizations of basic theological doctrines about heaven and hell, God and the devil, transgression, damnation, and redemption, and they were designed to inspire terror, awe, and dread. Wilde's audiences, on the other hand, were the beneficiaries of both the Enlightenment—which largely rejected these theological assumptions—and the Romantic period that followed it—a period during which the most terrifying supernatural figures of Christian theology—demons, gargoyles, and ghosts—were refashioned to accommodate regional folklore and the vast creative potential of the Gothic imagination.

Gothic Representations of the Alter Ego

The first Gothic romance is said to have been Horace Walpole's *The Castle of Otranto*, published in 1764, and the genre flourished throughout the 19th century in the works of writers such as Mary Shelley, E.T.A. Hoffmann, Charles Dickens, Bram Stoker, Edgar Allen Poe, Samuel Taylor Coleridge, Henry James, and Robert Louis Stevenson. Novelists such as Stephen King and Daphne du Maurier carried the Gothic standard into the 20th century, where its popularity shows no signs of abating.

The Gothic romance always aims to induce extreme emotions, foremost among them being terror, awe, and dread. These emotions are induced not by disclosing their object but by obscuring it in a place where reason cannot reach and all disbelief may be suspended, i.e., the supernatural, the paranormal, or the monstrous. This is the realm of the unconscious and the dream.

The dream, Freud declared, is the "royal road to the unconscious." Great literature, declares Girard, is the "gateway to the inner sanctum of the human drama." When these two great insights are conjoined, they point to the possibility of a literature informed by psychoanalysis—or preferably the reverse, as Girard insisted. Though Girard did not consider Gothic romances to be "great literature," they give shape and substance, if not lucidity, to products of the unconscious. Though they represent an aesthetic rather than any system of thought, they are analogous to the "manifest" content of dreams, as described by Freud. The dream's "latent" content, he believed, can only be accessed through analysis.

Like dreams, every story has both a manifest and a latent content. The challenge for literary analysis is bring the latent content into consciousness if the story itself has not already done so. Though Proust needed no help from either psychological or literary analysis, Gothic romances invite such analysis because of their obvious projections and substitutions. Like the dance of Salomé, they both obscure and reveal.

The unconscious mind—the sum of what the second and third brains do—doesn't give up its secrets easily. It protects the self from untimely exposures and brutal reckonings, and it enlists the services of the rational brain in doing so. Thus, it "rationalizes" story content by structuring it, even when that content is irrational and disorganized, as in dreams. Any coherent story must have a coherent structure, but that coherence will probably not map closely to the latent truth of the dream, the hallucination, or the pathology that inspired it. But the Gothic imagination was less interested in deciphering latent content than in offering rich representations of the manifest content. In the end, the project of decipherment was taken up by the rapidly developing human sciences, particularly psychiatry.

There can be no doubt that imaginative literature has historically enriched our understanding of the human experience. The Gothic imagination revealed dangerous and destructive intrapsychic forces not under our conscious control, defying the rationalist claims and aspirations of the Enlightenment. Whereas Catholicism had externalized these forces in the guise of demons and spirits, Gothic literature at least partially recognized their interiority, suggesting that they were nothing more than identifications, otherings, and projections. All these "others" were inside each of us, and they might even have started there. In Girardian terms, these frightening apparitions are among the others that constitute the self.

This kind of revelation can lead to wonderment or to dread, depending on one's ability to grasp it implications. Wilde's novel left the reader no way to imagine that Gray and the person depicted in his portrait were different, and his use of the painting as a metaphor for Gray's alter ego made that point hard to ignore. Though Freud had not yet formulated his theory of ego, superego, and id, the concept of an alter ego was familiar to readers of fiction in the 19th century. Alexandre Dumas' *The Count of Monte Cristo* (1844) is about an unjustly imprisoned man who escapes from prison and uses *three* alter egos to enact revenge against the men who put him there. Robert Louis Stevenson's *Dr Jekyll and Mr Hyde* appeared in 1886, four years before the publication of *Dorian Gray*. It, too, leaves no doubt about the identity of the shadow self.

Misrecognition of the Rival-Obstacle

Under extreme stress, an individual's sense of self can fragment into warring personalities facing off against each other. In these scenarios, especially where some form of abuse has occurred, the subject has internalized the rival Other and is attempting to expel or eliminate it.

It's always about how the subject experiences the rival—as an external threat, or as an internal one? As a serpent or as a part of the body? As an alternate body or an alternate self? The combinatorial possibilities are limited by the first brain, which supplies justifications for second- and third-brain responses to the rival.

What all these pathologies have in common is their misrecognition of the rival-obstacle, who always appears disguised as either a phobia (something outside the body), a conversion symptom (fear of a part or a function of the body), or an intraphysical, extrapsychic, or intrapsychic Other (devils, ghosts, and internalized rival-obstacles, respectively). Phobias and conversion symptoms are neurotic, while the internalized rival-obstacles, or "shadow selves," are psychotic delusions.

All these pathologies originate in the third brain and are controlled by it. The first and second brains' contributions are subsidiary. The second brain stages these delusions and provides their emotional coloration; the first brain provides the narratives explaining them.

Neurotic symptoms conceal the identity of the rival by completely de-personalizing and objectifying it as an animal, place, situation, or afflicted body part.

Psychotic delusions rely on alter egos to represent the desires of the rival. This is not to say that alter egos are uniformly associated with psychosis. Any teenage boy who has identified with Superman knows the difference between himself and his ego ideal, who is not a rival but a model. Many, if not all, of us carry around alter egos that express some aspect of our personalities.

MY MULTITUDE

In my personal experience, these alter egos are a multitude. My third brain draws on them like a casting director scanning unemployed actors at the studio gates, and "I" hear their voices or imagine their movements only milliseconds after they are selected. They are memories, re-presentations of sensory impressions left from observing and interacting with other people all my life. They are bits of song, show tunes, lines from Shakespeare, styles of public speaking, gestures and facial expressions borrowed from parents, teachers, and actors. They *only* appear spontaneously—never at my behest. If I try to consciously summon them, they don't show up. It may be John Gielgud for serious pronouncements, Maggie Smith for cutting ironies, and John Cleese for sententious remarks, though Slim Pickins and Andy Griffith sometimes show up when I'm feeling down-home.

Our stock of personas increases dramatically when we learn another language, for fluency requires a very high degree of openness (susceptibility) to the modeling of much more than grammar and phonetics. One cannot be for long immersed in another culture without adding untold numbers of "quotations" to one's database of voices, gestures, expressions, and attitudes.

This entire process, which I consider universal and refuse to call a "syndrome," rolls out unconsciously in most cases, though professional impersonators understand it well and can set it in motion at will. Each of *my* voices is that of someone whose behavior has been imprinted in my memory for "me" to imitate. Were I asked to identify a part of my self that is uniquely and authentically "me"—i.e., the imitating subject, I doubt I could find one. I am a composite of thousands of influences and thousands of desires, most of which I can't even remember or identify. The only thing unique about me or anyone is the particular way these desires are processed and assembled by my brain—or rather, the parts of it that I don't share with others.

This is what the psychotic cannot acknowledge, for, by definition, s/he has declared the anteriority and uniqueness of hisr desires over those of a model-rival who claims them for hisr own and denies the legitimacy of others' claims to them.

In what follows, I will illustrate and comment upon six alter ego scenarios, which I have characterized as either statistically normal and unproblematic, destructive, disturbing, sequestered, undetected, or temporary. I must emphasize that these categories overlap in some cases and that each instance of a pathology rolls out in a different environment. Also, these scenarios are, I will admit, reductive, but their purpose is to erect a scaffolding for further thought and understanding. Some of them are based on film characters such as *Birdman* or *Dorian Gray*, but it is Oughourlian's work on the mimetic brain that has inspired my rough groupings.

Statistically Normal

SCENARIO

"Wow! Birdman is my favorite superhero. He's smart and strong, and he always triumphs over his

enemies. I wish I could be like him and just jump into the air and take off. I really like how he rescues people in trouble and rounds up the bad guys and all. When Comic-con comes around this year, I'm planning to go as Birdman. I wish I could fly around like he does. That would really impress them!"

COMMENTARY

The subject admires Birdman, whom he understands to be a fictional character possessing all the superpowers that he himself would like to possess. He refers to Birdman as "he," never as "I" and makes no claims on Birdman's identity. He would like to become a superhero too, but since that's impossible, he'll eventually find ways to be a hero in everyday life.

The fictional character's mediation is external, for the subject knows that he is fictional and never regards him as a rival or an obstacle—only an ego ideal who inspires him to fight for truth and justice.

Self-Destructive

SCENARIO

"I am Birdman. I kid you not! I have amazing abilities like telekinesis and levitation. I can even fly when I want to. Okay, okay, I'm not performing for you now, because (sh-h-h!) someone is shadowing me. For real! He's impersonating me and stealing my very thoughts. He claims he is Birdman and that I am impersonating him! I can hear his voice, taunting me, daring me to prove that I'm really Birdman. He has some kind of power over me, like a power to make me feel really depressed and suicidal. I guess there's only one way I can prove to him and everyone else—including myself—that I am all that I claim to be! I'll fly through

the window and into the air! Everyone will look up from the streets below and shout, 'It's Birdman!'"

COMMENTARY

Here, the model's mediation has become internalized and is felt to be adversarial. What began as admiration has turned to rivalry and resentment, for the subject despairs of ever *being* Birdman, and he blames Birdman rather than himself for this impossibility. The more his self-image contradicts his fantasies, the more desperate he is to suppress that image and appropriate Birdman's essence. In his manic moments, he imagines that he *is* Birdman, but when his mood swings toward depression, he imagines that he hears Birdman's voice taunting him, telling him what a loser he is. Only in his manic state can he silence the internalized superhero imposter once and for all and validate his claim.

Disturbing, Caused by Trauma

SCENARIO

"I was severely abused as a child. My father was a violent man. I can only ever remember being terrified of him. He took out his rage and frustrations on my body and I was powerless to resist him. The only way I could cope was to imagine he was assaulting someone else, not me. My mother turned a blind eye to everything, and the abuse lasted for many years before he died."

I know he hurt me in ways that I'll never understand. I have trouble feeling anything, and sometimes when I look in a mirror, I can't find my reflection. I see that stranger—always the same one. Sometimes I look up and see him in the room with me. I'm sure he has stolen my body and is trying to take over the rest of me."

COMMENTARY

The subject's claims to his own body have encountered an powerful and terrifying obstacle—his father's claims to ownership of it. Unable to resist his father's assaults, the subject's self has split into two parts—one that he can still own and another that he must surrender. He then otherizes the second one—the suffering body. Being no longer his, it can cause him no more pain.

The subject's hallucinations are a first-brain capitulation to his second and third brains. Though the first brain is the "rational brain," its powers are restrained by the emotive and mimetic brains, which must at all costs protect the "real self" from ever being overtaken by the subject's otherized body—the body of pain. When he looks in the mirror, he sees a body that is not his, and because his father owns it, it must have malevolent intent.

It's worth repeating that the so-called "rational" brain doesn't always output rational explanations for incoming sense data. On the contrary, the rational brain is usually a handmaiden to the other two brains, which lean heavily into it when the need arises. This is in some ways fortunate, because the self's unity is not always an asset when it is being assaulted. Splitting off in the way the subject has done must be adaptive, since it allows him to continue functioning until he can become fully conscious of what has happened and deal with it effectively.

Out-of-body experiences take many forms. Hospital patients sometimes report floating above their own bodies, looking down. In such cases, the patient's self is dissociating from hisr body in order to protect itself from pain and death, as if saying, "That's not me lying there. I'm up here where everything is fine." The floating sensation suggests euphoria brought on by a medication. Even without the medications, though, this phenomenon is more common than we may imagine. Soldiers report experiencing it in wartime, which is hardly surprising considering that ownership of their bodies is taken from them during training. Unsurprisingly, victims of rape also report such reactions.

Sequestered

SCENARIO

"I'm disturbed by what I see in the mirror. I've lost my innocence and my face is beginning to show the traces of my secret libertine lifestyle. I know my

respectable friends sometimes find me cold-hearted, but they must never suspect how cruel I can actually be. All that is just a part of myself that I cannot

change, and I take no responsibility for it, though I try to shield it from scrutiny. I don't want it exposed."

I must spare no effort to cultivate a public image of decency, rectitude, and virtue. But I cannot renounce these troublesome desires and will find a space to give them free rein—a space outside or on the edges of the city where my respectable friends never venture and I can assume another identity."

COMMENTARY

The subject has resisted socialization and is not ready to abandon his pursuit of prohibited pleasures. Instead, he will keep his antisocial activities in the shadows. But concealment only gives his dark side scope to grow stronger with every passing year. The dark side is in fact associated with death—social death terminating eventually in actual death.

ALTERNATE SCENARIO

"When I look into the mirror, I see a homosexual, a fairy, a fag. It revolts me. I'm an abomination in the eyes of the Lord. I despise that part of me, but I can't seem to control it. It's like some sort of rogue personality inhabiting my body. I just have to make sure it doesn't show. Maybe it'll go away if I practice acting and dressing straight. Or maybe I can indulge it from time to time without getting found out. But it will never satisfy my desires, because I do not desire to be gay. Homosexuals disgust me."

COMMENTARY

The subject's self is splitting under the pressure of a social prohibition with which he cannot possibly comply without sacrificing his authentic, biologically-given sexual being. He splits into two selves—one that is gay and one that hates the first one. They will be at war with each other until cultural circumstances become more favorable to reunification. Until then, he can only heal his psychic splitting by coming "out" to everyone, thereby increasing the risk that he'll be persecuted. He will need support to heal the rift between his two selves.

Undetected, Unconscious

SCENARIO

(Based on the 1950 film noir, *Where the Sidewalk Ends*)

"I'm an honest police detective, but I despise the criminal class. My own father was a thief, so, believe me, I know that world. I've had several reprimands for roughing up suspects, but that's sometimes the only way to get their attention, if you know what I mean.

I guess I went too far recently: I punched a guy in the kisser and he fell over and died. It really wasn't my fault, but I knew it could look that way, so I denied any involvement with the guy and let somebody else take the rap. Hey, that's what it takes to clean up this city!"

COMMENTARY

The subject's departed father is his rival and obstacle. At some point, the subject has realized that his father's influence on him must be purged—othered and expelled—if he hopes ever to find his place in a law-abiding community. But his upbringing has given him few resources for the task, and whenever he thinks he has dealt with his father, the father returns under a new guise to reassert himself.

The son cannot cast out his father because his father has already imprinted certain behaviors and values on him. The son has learned under his father's tutelage to handle conflict with retributive violence, but he fails to recognize that his motivations and responses are not his own and that he is still under his father's spell.

Like the two Droogs at the end of *A Clockwork Orange,* he has chosen a profession that will allow him to pursue and brutalize criminals. In every one of them, he sees the father that he hates.

The subject's rationalizations excusing his own criminality are a sign that his rational brain has been commandeered by his mimetic and emotional brains.

Temporary and Induced (Hypnotism)

Where "positive" reciprocity occurs, the two vectors of suggestion and imitation in the mimetic triangle (the interdividual rapport) are not in conflict. What is modeled is imitated, not rejected.

Where there is negative reciprocity, the subject rejects the suggestion, and the model imitates the rejection, simultaneously modeling rejection for the subject, who then imitates the model's rejection with a third one of hisr own. Each individual believes s/he is rejecting the other' influence, but in reality, each is imitating the other's rejection of influence. This back-and-forth movement of negative desire produces a hostile, rivalrous relationship.

Hypnosis immobilizes the interdividual rapport before it becomes rivalrous. The hypnotist, by instilling trust, locks that rapport into one position—that of positive reciprocity—allowing him nearly unrestricted access to the subject's mimetic control center. With that power, the hypnotist fashions a new self for the subject—one that will be neither conscious of the former self nor remembered by it when the session ends. Until then, the new self is empty of everything except the hypnotist's desires and is formed solely by imitating them.

Therapeutic applications of hypnosis have been highly successful in treating a variety of psychological disorders because they induce the subject to let go of everything except the present moment. Similar effects can be produced through meditation and certain psychoactive substances such as cannabis, LSD and psilocybin.

Phaedra

One of the most powerful and ubiquitous taboos found throughout human societies has concerned incest between a young man and the females in his immediate family—his sisters and his mother or stepmother. This taboo exists for a number of biological and socio-economic reasons that have only recently been identified, such as the risk of inbreeding or failing to form ties with other families through marriage.

Mimetic theory looks primarily at the danger of highly volatile rivalries within the nuclear family, the basic unit of society. Incest between a son and his mother or stepmother is a dagger plunged into the heart of his father and is sure to bring about a catastrophic and irreversible rupture in family relations. No legend illustrates this better than the ancient tale of Phaedra, her husband Theseus, and her stepson Hippolytus, which has inspired two dozen plays or poems and ten films. The film I would like to examine is Jules Dassin's *Phaedra* (1962), an adaptation of Euripides' *Hippolytus*. It stars Melina Mercouri, Anthony Perkins, and Raf Vallone.

ASCENT

In the film's version of the tale, the father, Thanos, is a Greek shipping magnate whose son, Alexis, has been raised abroad by his mother, Thanos' estranged first wife. Thanos wants him to return to Greece and learn to manage the company. He sends his current wife, Phaedra, to Paris to meet Alexis and invite him for the summer. In Paris, Alexis and Phaedra hit it off right away, each succumbing to the other's charms.

Alexis introduces her to his "girlfriend," an expensive Italian sports car displayed in a Paris showroom. The implication is clear that a negotiation between him and his father has begun, with Phaedra as an ally and go-between. She happily accepts this role, as she, like her husband, wants to lure Alexis back to Greece.

Nothing stokes intense desire more than an intractable obstacle. During the short interval before her return home, Phaedra's fascination with Alexis becomes an all-consuming passion—the kind that develops when an unsurmountable barrier separates the subject from the desired object. For now, this obstacle is the incest taboo, as symbolized by the father, and there is no reason to believe that Alexis's desire is not also energized by it. But Alexis is a playboy who already plays fast and loose with the rules and shows little interest in commitment. His infatuation with Phaedra, though strong, may reach its climax in the same moment that he succeeds in seducing her. Her passion, on the other hand, may not subside as easily as his.

But the trajectory of their illicit love is interrupted by her return to Greece. At this point, Alexis seems much more interested in possessing the sports car and his father's wife than in inheriting his father's company. But returning to Greece will be the price he has to pay for both her and the car, and so he happily returns there. Thanos welcomes him with open arms and roasts the fatted calf. Some days later, the sports car arrives on one of the ships and Alexis tries it out along the winding mountain roads nearby.

It must be noted that Thanos loves Phaedra passionately and treats her like a queen. He even names one of his ships after her. For her part, she shows no signs of being unhappy with him. In all that follows, she never blames him for anything.

DESCENT

Left alone together one evening after Alexis's return, he and Phaedra are overcome by desire and make passionate love. But their passion is soon overshadowed by fear and dread over what they have done, and Alexis considers returning to London immediately. But he stays, and the tensions between him and Phaedra begin to escalate in tandem with their mounting guilt. Nevertheless, Phaedra finds she cannot give Alexis up and begins to pursue him, consequences be damned. He is ambivalent at first, then pleads with her to let him go. She refuses to do so and, instead, keeps the pressure on.

Phaedra, a beautiful and proud woman, is now a scorned woman whose desire oscillates between fascination with the man who has spurned her and bitter hatred toward him.

At a large social gathering of mostly shipping families, Alexis is introduced to Ercy, the daughter of another rich industrialist who also owns a fleet of ships. Her father and Thanos hope for a merger of their companies *and* their families through an arranged marriage between Alexis and Ercy. In fact, Ercy is smitten with Alexis, though he reciprocates by seducing another girl right under her nose. When Ercy reproaches him for this behavior, he reproaches her in turn for attempting to limit his freedom, then makes a half-hearted effort to woo her back without offering an apology. This obviously sets a bad tone for their forthcoming marriage.

Whereas Ercy's intentions are pure, Alexis's bad faith betrays his absence of commitment to her. And yet, he will not cast her aside as he has done to Phaedra, for he has embraced his father's vision for him. He will marry Ercy and follow in Thanos's footsteps.

Nothing about these new developments pleases Phaedra, whose only child by Thanos—a boy of about 10—will no longer be in line for ownership of the company. Worst of all, she will lose Alexis to Ercy.

In Phaedra's mind, all this adds up to disempowerment and defeat—a narcissistic deflation of huge proportions. Perhaps she fears that Thanos and the villagers will no longer treat her as a queen, that she will be "replaced" by a younger woman. Furthermore, her stepson will no longer be an ally and will watch her age and become irrelevant.

Phaedra's fears of aging, irrelevance, and death are no different than Margo Channing's in *All About Eve*. (See my review in Chapter 2.) But, whereas Margo is eventually able to break the spell that Eve has over her, Phaedra is unwilling or unable to undergo such a transformation. In her case, that would involve letting Alexis go and accepting the reality of her circumstances.

I would hasten to add that her circumstances are quite different from Margo's, for she is a Greek woman living in a culture that has, for millennia, modeled only one fate for women who violate the incest taboo—and that fate is death, preferably by suicide. Phaedra probably sees that coming but cannot let go of her obsession with Alexis, who is now not just the object of her desire but also an additional obstacle to it. Given that desire thrives on obstacles and that there are now two of them, Phaedra is now at the point where Margo was when she famously said, "Fasten your seatbelts. It's gonna be a bumpy ride."

CATASTROPHE

Phaedra determines not to allow the marriage to happen, and warns Alexis that she will expose both him and herself if he does not comply with her wishes. In a highly charged showdown between them on the landing just outside a room Thanos and some friends are playing cards, Alexis and Phaedra come perilously close to a public disclosure of their affair. Alexis is the one who flinches, and Phaedra appears to be the one in control.

She is in fact holding Alexis's entire fate hostage as long as she is willing to destroy everything—including him, his father, the company, and herself—if he thwarts her desire.

The total destruction commences the following morning, when news arrives that one of the company's ships, the one christened "Phaedra," has broken up on the shoals of a North Sea island. Nearly a hundred crew members are reported dead, and their grieving mothers and widows, all in black—the "chorus" of this Greek tragedy—have cascaded down the steps from the town and are now massed in the hallway outside the office where Thanos, Alexis, and company officials are assembled. All are grieving and in a state of shock.

Then, into the crowd of mourning women in black walks Phaedra, wearing a white dress and turban with dark glasses. Pushing her way rudely through the crowd of women, she enters the adjoining office. There, she instructs an employee to summon her husband. When Thanos appears, she coldly informs him that Alexis is her lover, then leaves.

The scene that follows is incendiary. Thanos orders Alexis into the room and immediately assaults him both verbally and physically, delivering blow after blow to his face. Alexis's reaction is to reproach his father for having brought him back to Greece, in effect saying, "This is all your fault." Thanos then commands him to leave Greece and never return.

When we next see Alexis, he is bathing his wounds under a faucet in the garage near his car. He is no longer proud and confident. His sense of himself has utterly collapsed, for he has been banished and is in the throes of social death. He takes his car out and opens it up on the mountain roads overlooking the sea. There, he hears a siren song in Bach's Organ Toccata in F Major, playing on his car radio at full volume. Shouting

Phase One: The Ascent

Note: The interdividual relations modeled by these four triangles are *simultaneous*.

Subject	Modeling	Obstruction
Alexis	**A** Phaedra (O); Alexis (S); M 1. Thanos as Phaedra's adoring husband 2. Phaedra as narcissist	**B** Phaedra (O); Alexis (S); Obs 1. Thanos 2. The incest taboo
Phaedra	**C** Alexis (O); Phaedra (S); M 1. Alexis as narcissist 2. His female admirers and others	**D** Alexis (O); Phaedra (S); Obs 1. Thanos 2. The incest taboo

Figure 20: The Ascent

Phaedra's name, he loses (or surrenders?) control of the car and crashes on the rocks below.

His body is brought back to his father's house. Phaedra is alone upstairs with her maid who, faithful to the end, assists her in dying from a drug overdose.

IMBRICATIONS

The *Phaedra* legend as Dassin has interpreted it yields easily to a mimetic analysis revealing not just one

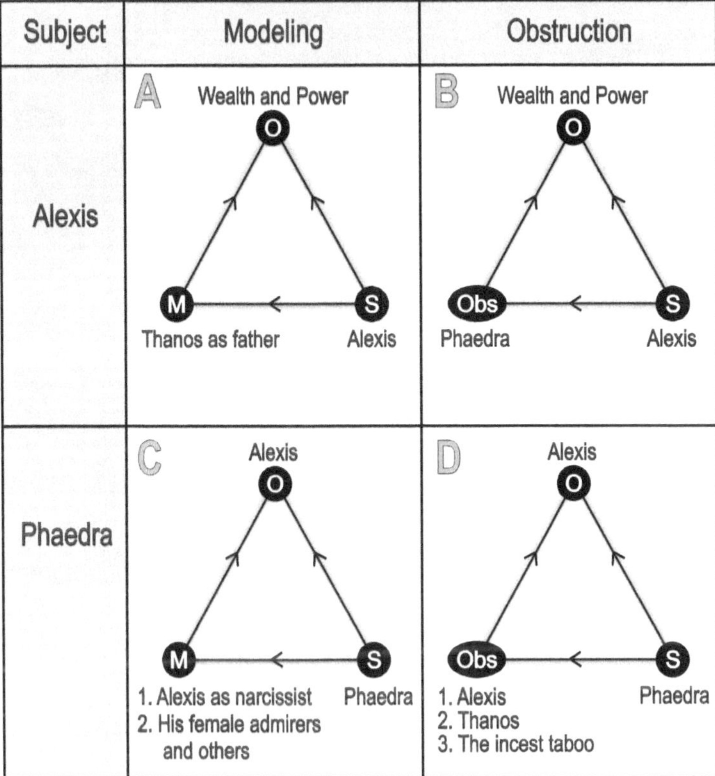

Figure 21: The Descent

triangle, but many, locked together in a dance of desire and death. Like latticed crystal formations, these movements of desire follow certain predictable patterns, as if the players had no control over their own fates and were carried along by some sort of mechanical stage machinery. This is why Girardians call these patterns of movement the "mechanisms of desire," and Oughourlian refers to the players as "puppets of desire."

The action in *Phaedra* can be divided into two phases which I have called the "ascent" (pre-coitus) and the "descent" (post-coitus). In each of these phases, the principal "subjects" are Alexis and Phaedra, but their desires are modeled and obstructed by different players as the action progresses from the first to the second phase.

In the first phase, each of them is fascinated by the other. This fascination cannot be described as "love," for neither of them desires what is best for the other. Instead, they are drawn together by their narcissism and the desires of third-party models. In Phaedra's case, the third parties are all those who desire or dote on Alexis, and in Alexis's case, the principal third party is Thanos, who adores Phaedra and treats her like a queen. But Thanos is also in love with his company and models his own ambitions for Alexis to imitate. However, in saying to Alexis, "Be like me. Desire what I desire and inherit the company," Thanos perhaps unwittingly incites Alexis's desire for Phaedra.

As I think I've shown, desire is energized by rivalry and obstruction. In the Genesis story, God's prohibition against eating the fruit of a designated tree makes the tree appear more desirable than all the others. For Phaedra and Alexis, the incest taboo is an equivalent prohibition—one that their hubris leads them to believe they can flout with impunity. The manic euphoria that accompanies their narcissism is then multiplied by the euphoria that they experience as lovers, leading them to disregard and thus "overcome" the prohibition-obstacle.

Reality asserts itself the morning after. They have not truly "overcome" the prohibition. They have only violated it, and remorse and guilt set in.

In the second phase (the "descent"), we see a decisive shift in the movements of desire. The object of

Alexis's desire is no longer Phaedra. He has found other objects and wants to move on.

Phaedra, for her part, desires Alexis more than ever because he has spurned her and become—like his father, the incest taboo, and Ercy—one more insuperable obstacle. Desire, resentment, and hatred make a volatile mix. The manic narcissism that drove her passion for possession of the object (Alexis) now drives her passion for its destruction.

She will confess to her husband and let events take their course. She knows what course they will take.

Conclusion

My hope in writing this book has been to introduce mimetic theory to a wider audience than it has so far enjoyed, at least in the US where I live. Since the theory grew out of the rich soil of the French intellectual tradition, most of the earlier writings were Eurocentric. Girard's earliest focus was on great European novels by Stendhal, Proust, Flaubert, Cervantes, and Dostoyevsky. Because my education had also been very Eurocentric, these novels were already familiar to me and provided a good "leg up" to the theory.

I suspect that many Americans who have never read any of these authors shy away from the theory because they don't expect to understand it. It has never been successfully popularized in the US, though Michigan University Press has published an impressive collection of scholarly studies of mimetic theory in its "Studies in Violence, Mimesis, and Culture" series. The scholars I read seemed to agree on the highly generative nature of the theory, measured by the number and variety of phenomena it explains as well as its ability to generate new explanations.

As I was introduced to mimetic theory during its early period (the seventies), I've had four decades to read further and absorb it. During those years, I've also consumed thousands of movies, hundreds of stage performances, and no small number of books. I've lived in several countries and experienced ups and downs in my personal relationships. Again and again, I've found the mimetic triangle to be a useful template for understanding interpersonal relationships whether lived or depicted. All relationships may be inscribed within the triangular model of desire, and all are scalable and generative of culture. All cultural institutions, whether in religion, law, education, or the arts, hang on the triangular scaffolding. My use of the word "all" is calculated to convey the universality of mimetic desire in human relationships.

In my research for this book, I found no dramatic or comedic narratives that could not be better understood by identifying their triangles, the occupants of the triangles' three corners, and the mimetic forces governing their interactions. The writers' or directors' own intuitions about mimesis may have ranged from strong to non-existent, but the triangles were always present in some form and integral to the action.

Because fictional narratives are about lived human experience, the most insightful ones have always been of the greatest interest to the human sciences—most notably, to sociology, psychology, anthropology, theories of religion, political science, and economics. Beginning in the 1990s, neuroscience has contributed greatly to our understanding of the biochemical processes underlying mimesis. This development has given psychologists like Jean-Michel Oughourlian scope for positing the existence of a "third (mimetic) brain" that is also the locus of the interdividual rapport (see Figure 1). This concept has proved its worth in helping us understand how powerful and determinative the mimetic brain can be with respect to our rational and emotive brains.

While writing this book, I realized more than ever that "I" am a multitude of others whose voices, gestures, goals and attitudes I've preserved in my random-access memory. Without them, "I" would never know what and what not to do or say. This is not an avoidance of responsibility, for my conscious brain is still the gatekeeper, the censor, the superego, and the decider. When it fails, I, like Phaedra and Alexis, am under the control of my unconscious—what Euripides might have called my "fate."

Index

About the Author

Doughlas Remy is the author of two other books about mimetic theory—*Things Hidden in Plain Sight: Mimesis and Human Violence* (2022), and *In the Beginning Was the Word: Mimesis, Violence, and the Origin of Language* (2023). He attended Louisiana State University and the University of Texas and earned graduate degrees in French, Italian, and Foreign Language Education. He lived for eleven years in the Middle East and returned to the US in 1990, settling in Seattle, Washington, where he worked until retirement in tech companies, community colleges, and at the University of Washington. He has also been an active and professional artist and graphic designer. His interest in mimetic theory dates back to 1978, when he attended a lecture by René Girard. He is a member of the Colloquium on Violence and Religion, founded in 1990 at Stanford University to explore, critique, and develop Girard's theory, and he has given numerous lectures on the theory in the Seattle area.

Email: doremiarts@live.com
Website: doremiarts.com

www.ingramcontent.com/pod-product-compliance
Lightning Source LLC
Chambersburg PA
CBHW051045250726
48656CB00001B/159